FAQs for NQTs

As trainee teachers make the transition from student to teacher, they face many issues that they didn't consider during their studies. Entering the classroom for the first time as a qualified teacher can be a daunting prospect, not only in terms of teaching the students, but also in terms of forging relationships with new colleagues and gaining professional support, advice and respect within the workplace. This useful handy reference book offers authoritative yet accessible answers to common questions posed by new and trainee teachers as they face these new experiences.

Organised into logical sections the book covers issues such as

- job hunting
- induction
- managing your workload
- relationship building with pupils and colleagues
- dealing with parents
- personal issues.

The frequently asked questions the book answers have all been highlighted through Elizabeth Holmes' work as an online agony aunt for teachers via her 'Ask Elizabeth' forum on Eteach.com as well as the feedback and queries she has received from readers of her other books for teachers. Based on real questions with common themes this will be a handy, reliable and confidence-building book for any new teacher to have on the shelf.

Elizabeth Holmes is a professional writer specialising in education. Among her many published works is the highly respected book *The Newly Qualified Teacher's Handbook*. She also writes a weekly newsletter for Eteach.com, as well as writing for and moderating its online staffroom, which is duplicated on a number of associated websites. In addition, Elizabeth is a freelance educational consultant contributing to the work of a number of specialist bodies including the Teacher Support Network and Optimus Professional Learning.

FAQs for NQTs

Practical advice and working solutions for newly qualified teachers

Elizabeth Holmes

Routledge
Taylor & Francis Group

LONDON AND NEW YORK

First published 2006 by Routledge
2 Park Square, Milton Park, Abingdon, Oxon OX14 4RN

Simultaneously published in the USA and Canada
by Routledge
270 Madison Ave, New York, NY 10016

*Routledge is an imprint of the Taylor & Francis Group,
an informa business*

© 2006 Elizabeth Holmes

Typeset in Garamond and Gill by BC Typesetting Ltd, Bristol
Printed and bound in Great Britain by
TJ International Ltd, Padstow, Cornwall

British Library Cataloguing in Publication Data
A catalogue record for this book is available from the British Library

Library of Congress Cataloging in Publication Data
Holmes, Elizabeth, 1969–
     FAQs for NQTs: practical advice and workable solutions for
newly qualified teachers/Elizabeth Holmes.
         p. cm.
     ISBN 0–415–36795–6 (hardback) – ISBN 0–415–36796–4 (pbk.)
     1. First-year teachers. 2. Teaching. I. Title.
     LB2844.1.N4H649   2006
     371.1–dc22
2005031141

ISBN10: 0–415–36795–6 (hbk)
ISBN10: 0–415–36796–4 (pbk)
ISBN10: 0–203–02741–8 (ebk)

ISBN13: 978–0–415–36795–0 (hbk)
ISBN13: 978–0–415–36796–7 (pbk)
ISBN13: 978–0–203–02741–7 (ebk)

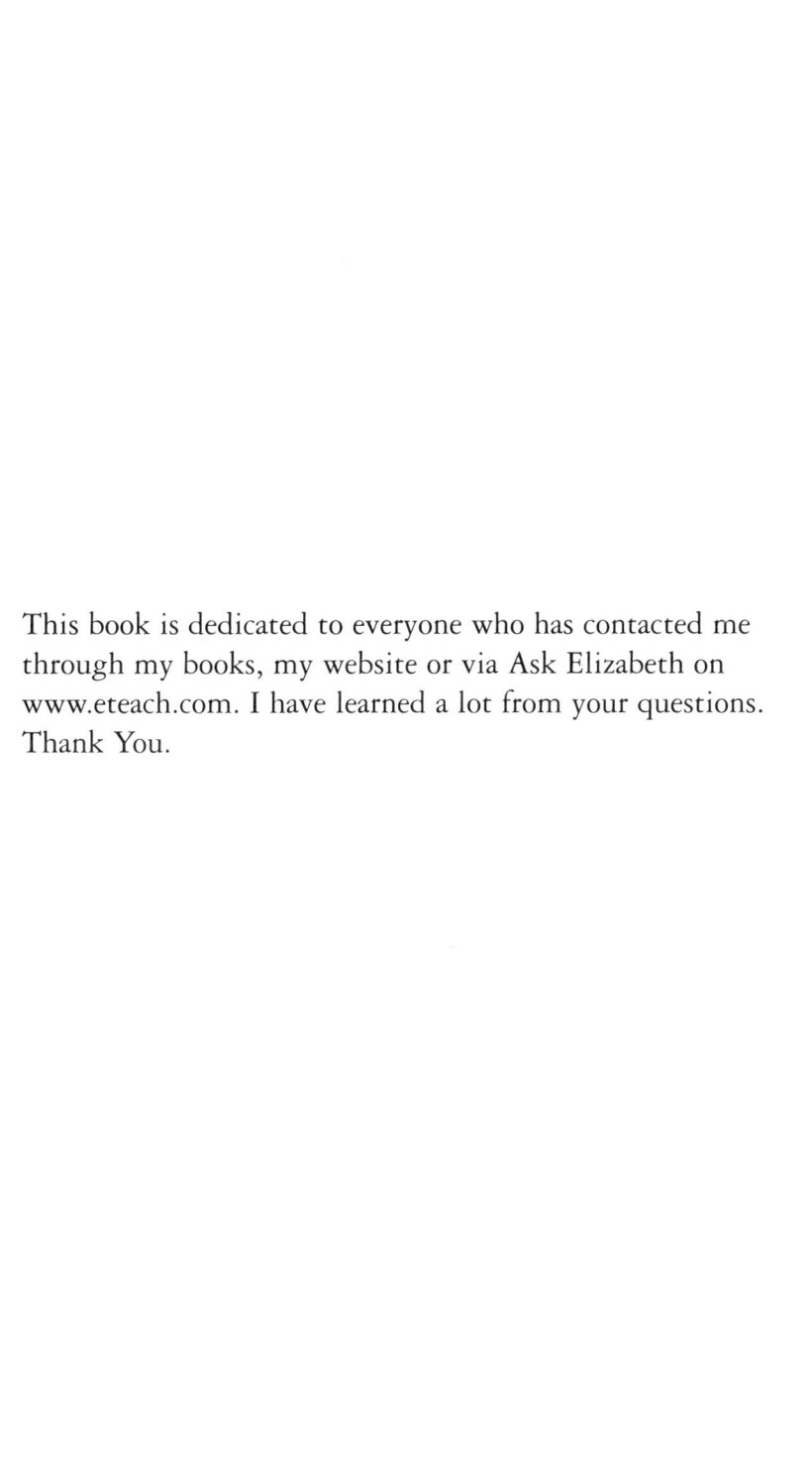

This book is dedicated to everyone who has contacted me through my books, my website or via Ask Elizabeth on www.eteach.com. I have learned a lot from your questions. Thank You.

Contents

Acknowledgements

My thanks go to Philip Mudd, Kerry Maciak and Fiona Wade of Routledge and Charlotte Howard of Fox and Howard Literary Agency. I'm very grateful for your support and encouragement. In addition, I would like to thank everyone who has asked the questions over the last six years, and the many people in various government departments and agencies, websites and unions who have helped me to answer them. At times, it's certainly a team effort!

Introduction

Since the publication of *The Newly Qualified Teacher's Handbook*, and taking on the role of online agony aunt for newly qualified teachers (NQTs) on the teacher recruitment website www.eteach.com, I have been asked countless questions about the finer details of the first few years in the teaching profession. Everything from interview nerves to first day jitters, induction observations to managing stress and much more has been covered in questions from NQTs and soon-to-be NQTs. While some of those asked have been straightforward to answer, others have been intractable and complex, requiring ongoing support and, in some cases, extensive research to resolve.

I believe that the fact that so many questions are asked is not in any way down to shortcomings in the quality of initial teacher training. An immense amount is covered during training and there are bound to be questions left unasked and unanswered. If this book can contribute to clearing up the classic uncertainties that new teachers may have it will have achieved its intentions.

Most of the questions answered in this book are equally applicable to both primary and secondary teachers, and have been chosen specifically to convey information as well as to blast through many of the common misconceptions that exist out there. While your specific question(s) may not appear here precisely, those that are covered should help to trigger in you the start of a solution or the first steps towards a resolution for any issues that you face as an NQT. If this is not the case, or if the questions posed and answered have given rise to further questions in your mind, you can visit the Eteach.com online staffroom to pose them in the Ask Elizabeth section of the NQT and Student Zone (see www.eteach.com for further details). Remember, questions, issues, anxieties and concerns can all be fantastic opportunities for growth, development and learning.

If readers take just one clear message from any of my books for new teachers I'd like it to be this: that you *never* have to struggle on alone if you are experiencing difficulties. There is *always* someone who will be in a position to help you, whether that's your induction tutor or mentor in school, the person with responsibilities for NQTs within your local education authority (LEA), your union, advisers at the Department for Education and Skills (DfES) or General Teaching Council (GTC), this book, or contributors to online teaching staffrooms such as that found at www.eteach.com. Never leave concerns to gather strength and debilitate you; *always* seek help sooner rather than later. You wouldn't be the first and you certainly won't be the last! These sources of help are not faceless, nameless bureaucrats who care nothing about the plight of the new teacher; they are genuinely helpful and go out of their way to ensure that queries are dealt with efficiently and effectively. Don't feel as though the DfES, and its equivalents around the UK, is unapproachable, or is some distant administrative authority that cares nothing for those on the frontline. That simply isn't the case in my experience.

The second most important thing to take on board is the degree of enjoyment there is to be had from a teaching career. Undoubtedly it's busy, at times stressful and invariably demanding, but there's a lot of fun in it as well as rich experience to come from working with such an incredible range of people and ages. Be sure to allow yourself time to acknowledge that.

Latest information

The teaching profession is organic and dynamic and, as you'll no doubt be aware, changes can occur with relative frequency. Although the information in this book is correct at the time of going to press, the further information boxes included carry the websites and phone numbers from which the latest updates can be sourced.

I like to think that the books that I write are works in progress and the feedback that I receive from readers greatly helps to inform the changes and developments that these books go through over time. If you feel that there are any questions that aren't covered in this book that should be, you can email your suggestions to me: eh@elizabethholmes.co.uk.

Author's note

The advice given in this book is for information and guidance only and is not intended to replace that of qualified practitioners. In particular, if a reader is experiencing adverse health symptoms, expert advice from a fully qualified health care practitioner should be sought. Symptoms of stress, especially, require careful management, and while self-help techniques can help tremendously, it is always wise to seek expert advice. Neither the author nor the publisher can be held responsible for any consequences that occur as a result of following the guidance contained herein.

CHAPTER I

Job hunting

There is nothing which persevering effort and unceasing and diligent care cannot accomplish.

(Seneca)

Introduction

There's a certain irony in the fact that just as you're in the thick of the stresses and strains of school placements and what seems like the astonishing workload they generate, combined with coursework and the inevitable coughs and colds that you're susceptible to as you battle legions of bugs delighted at the prospect of a fresh new host, this is also precisely the time you could be pulling out all the stops in your hunt for a job. While in an ideal world you'd be able to draw your training course to a close, take a well-earned break and then gently start to think about your next steps in your career, it just isn't like that in reality unless you want to face the panic of realising that all your mates have a job for September and you don't!

The hunt for a job needn't be the potential nightmare it can seem if you devote time to a little forward planning and attention to detail. Knowing when, how and where to look for the perfect vacancy, in combination with the ability to be patient, is all it takes. Oh, and a positive mental attitude can help too. Things may not happen as quickly as you'd like them to, but the more upbeat you can remain, the easier you will make it for yourself.

This chapter explores the typical questions that soon to be newly qualified teachers ask as they launch themselves into their hunt for employment. If this applies to you, take it one step at a time, be thorough and committed, and sell yourself with pride! Good luck!

FAQs in this chapter cover:

- When to look for work
- Fast Track
- Switching from primary to secondary and vice versa
- Finding job vacancies
- Working in the independent sector
- Medical fitness to teach
- Not getting a job
- Working in a faith school
- Using qualified teacher status (QTS) elsewhere
- Making speculative applications
- Supporting statements
- Referees and references
- LEA pools
- Training and teaching in England and Wales
- Interview nerves
- Interview questions
- Asking questions in interviews
- Portfolios
- Finding accommodation
- Visiting your school before starting work
- Contracts
- Joining a union

Help! I haven't got a job

When should I start looking for work?

It's a good idea to start looking any time from January in the year that you'll qualify. If you start too early you may be tempted to fall into the first job you see when it may not be totally suitable for you. Leave it too late though, and you'll start to panic. Aim to search at a steady pace so that you have time to devote to making applications. Don't forget that you don't have to wait until a job is advertised to apply for it. If you know the area or school that you want to work in, send in your CV and a covering letter as a speculative application. You never know when it might land on the right desk at an opportune time!

See: Making speculative applications on page 11.

I've heard about the Fast Track but don't know if I should be going for it. How can I find out more?

Recent changes have been made to the Fast Track Teaching programme which mean that it is no longer recruiting trainees – only qualified teachers in the early stages of their careers. The guidance on this programme states that the Fast Track teachers are 'the kind of people who welcome additional responsibilities and who are committed to improving educational standards in schools through effective leadership'. The aim is that teachers on the programme will be ready for leadership positions in education within five years. If this sounds like you, it would be well worth finding out more from the Fast Track website (see below).

You can find out all you need to know about the Fast Track programme from the following website: www.fasttrackteaching.gov.uk.

What if I decide that I want to teach secondary after training for the primary sector?

This needn't be a problem. There is no legal requirement in England to retrain if you want to switch phases (from primary to secondary or secondary to primary). QTS is QTS so you can teach right through from primary to secondary, and in theory, any subject too. That said, you may want to do some voluntary work in a secondary school just to gain experience, and some LEAs and training providers offer conversion courses that may be of interest. One thing to keep in mind is that you are likely to find it easier to get a job within your specialist areas, and the induction guidelines do suggest that it is best completed within the phase and subject area in which you have been trained. Doing this would certainly make for an easier life than switching phases so soon. Unless you know that there is no way you will teach in a primary school, I'd suggest getting your induction out of the way and then thinking about making the switch.

Where can I find all the job vacancies?

There is no single source of all teaching vacancies so you will have to spread your search to include as many possible sources as you can. Your ideal job is going to be advertised somewhere and if you're not looking in the right places you'll miss out!

Things have changed in the world of teaching job vacancies over recent years and now the most likely place to find vacancies listed is on the internet on specialist teaching vacancy sites such as www. eteach.com.

Some unions have internet-based job clubs too which may be hosting your ideal vacancy, and local education authorities often publish vacancies on line and in paper-based job bulletins.

The local press will carry local teaching vacancies. If you plan to be moving to a new area see if you can receive local newspapers through the post or ask if vacancies are posted online anywhere.

The national press sometimes carries teaching vacancies. All the broadsheets such as the *Guardian*, the *Independent*, *The Times* and the *Telegraph* have education supplements covering news and jobs.

In summary you need to be looking:

- first and foremost online at specialist and dedicated teaching job sites such as www.eteach.com
- at your union's website
- at the websites of the local education authorities that you'd like to work in
- at any paper-based LEA bulletins that are relevant to you

- in the local press and related websites
- in the national press.

Remember that there will be natural increases in the numbers of jobs advertised following the typical resignation dates through the academic year: end of October, end of February and end of May.

Finally, don't underestimate the power of networking! The contacts that you make during your teaching placements may well lead to permanent work so keep your eyes and ears open and don't be afraid to let schools know if you would like a job there.

I'm thinking of working in an independent school. What do I need to take into consideration?

The biggest consideration when thinking about working in the independent sector is whether or not you would be able to complete your induction period in a particular school. It is possible to do induction in independent schools but only under certain circumstances, so you would need to get this checked out by the school. Be sure to get it in writing if you are told that induction can be completed there *before* making any applications.

Other important considerations concern your pay, your pension entitlements, the degree of job security offered, the curriculum covered and the type of contract that you would have. Individual independent schools would have to answer all of these questions, but you can find generic advice and information concerning member schools on the Independent Schools Council (ISC) website: www.isc.co.uk.

I've been epileptic since I was a teenager although this is totally controlled by medication. Now I've been asked to complete a 'health details' form for a job. Will they automatically assume that I'm not fit to teach because of my epilepsy? I'm not sure what to put on the form.

I strongly advise you to be open about your condition, but you may also like to add details such as the date of your last seizure (to show that these are not happening regularly) and how effectively the condition is managed. Your general practitioner (GP) may also write an open letter to whom it may concern about the impact that the condition has on your working life. All of this evidence is useful in addressing the concerns that some employers may have. The more information you offer, the better it will look.

> The general principle here is honesty. Whatever issue or ailment you may have that you feel may hinder your search for a job, be open and honest about it but dress it in the most positive way possible. Never be tempted to hide or conceal anything that schools should know about or take into consideration, but there's nothing wrong with emphasising the positive!

I'm finding it really hard to get a job. It's late June already and so far I've made eight applications and had two interviews but still nothing. It's not as if there are loads of jobs for me to go for in my area. I'm really starting to panic – what can I do?

Make sure you're looking for vacancies in the right places. Schools are using a range of methods to advertise, and you have to be covering all the bases to make sure that you don't miss out. Most vacancies are advertised online now and many LEAs will publish job bulletins on their own websites. It's possible to complete an online CV on www.eteach.com that employers can browse. Eteach also has a Permanent Placement Team working to find schools the candidates they need so it's worth giving them a ring (0845 226 1905). You can also make speculative applications as well as talking to the recruitment managers that work in LEAs. The wider you can make your search the better. If you're restricted to one area it may take longer, but don't be tempted to dash to the other end of the country to chase a job if you know that you'll be miserable far away from your family and friends. The induction period is too important and potentially challenging to add homesickness into the equation. Teaching vacancies crop up all through the academic year so even if you don't get something for a September start, the chances are you'll be in a job for the spring or summer terms. In the meantime, aim to gain as much experience as possible. If funds allow, do some voluntary work in a local school, as this is all good CV fodder. Consider going for temporary contracts too, as you never know what they may lead to. Stay positive; something will turn up!

I've got an interview in a faith school. Should I be prepared for questions on my religious beliefs?

Basically any interview in a faith or religious denominational school should be broadly similar to interviews in non-faith or community schools but you should expect to be asked *something* about your faith. Although there's no way of predicting what questions NQTs are asked in interviews, many going for jobs in faith schools do report having been asked questions along the following lines:

- What role do you see the church (whether Catholic, Church of England or other) having in the education of young people?
- What can schools do for the church?
- In what ways, specifically, can you support the religious ethos of the school?
- Do your beliefs complement those of the school? How can you demonstrate that?

In short, you need to be able to show that you have no philosophical objections to the religious work of and in the school and, in fact, that you will be able actively to support it. If you feel that this may be an issue for you, or even if you feel indifferent to the faith, it's probably not going to be a good idea to go for the job.

I have completed my training and successfully got QTS but I'm really not sure if teaching is for me. Can I use the qualification to do anything else?

A teaching qualification is evidence of a vast range of skills such as your ability to organise, to deploy people skills such as communication and negotiation, to work to tight deadlines and to work in a highly pressured environment. These skills are generally recognised and valued by professions and industries outside the world of teaching and you'll almost certainly find it relatively easy to transfer them to a new career. You might like to think about working in classroom resource development for a publisher, as an education officer within a charity or museum, in education administration, as a trainer in industry or in any form of caring work for children and young people. The possibilities really are endless so it's well worth doing your research and seeking some professional careers advice from your initial teacher training provider (university or college) or from your local careers office. Take a look in the Yellow Pages for further details on careers advice. Keep an open mind and aim to match as closely as possible the way you love to spend your time with possible career or job choices. A careers adviser will help you to achieve this.

However, all of that said, I do feel that it is usually best to stay in the teaching profession at least as long as it takes you to get your induction done and dusted so that should you ever decide to return to teaching at some later date, perhaps when your life circumstances have changed, you don't have to face the hurdle of completing induction years after you gained QTS. Unless you know that you really won't ever be venturing into the classroom again, think carefully about leaving before you have completed induction.

I haven't seen any vacancies that I want to go for but there is a school I'd be really keen to work in if a job ever came up. What should I do?

It's perfectly acceptable to make a speculative application that the head teacher can keep on file until he or she has a vacancy. It may not lead to immediate employment but at least you would be doing something proactive about finding a job!

The best way to go about it is to take the following steps:

- Find out exactly who your letter should be addressed to (usually the head teacher).
- Plan your letter carefully so that you keep it punchy and to the point, including only that which entices the reader into wanting to find out more. Include your achievements and outstanding skills and stick to just one side of A4.
- State the type of vacancy that you're interested in.
- Match your skills and experience to what you know of the school.
- State some attributes that you feel you can bring to the school (give examples where possible).
- Be bold in asking for an interview and state some possible dates that would suit you (don't be too specific here – saying something like 'I can be available to visit your school over the next few weeks' is fine).
- Get your CV up to date and glowing and include a copy with your letter.
- Be sure to use good quality paper and enclose a stamped addressed envelope.
- Make a follow-up call if you don't hear anything within a week or two.

You never know, your letter may land on someone's desk at the perfect moment so it's always worth giving speculative applications a go. Nothing ventured, nothing gained!

Is a letter of application the same as a supporting statement?

Essentially, yes, but you should take into consideration the fact that if a school asks for a letter of application they do actually mean for it to be laid out as a letter. If you have to complete a box (usually a page with the option to continue on a separate sheet of paper) in an application form it doesn't need to be presented as a letter (unless specified).

I'm really stuck on writing my supporting statement. How on earth do I go about it?

This is, without doubt, the trickiest part of the application process. Filling in boxes on forms about past qualifications is a mere breeze compared with the sweat and tears often associated with having to sell yourself. Maybe it's a cultural thing!

That said, following these steps can take a good deal of the pain out of the process:

- Always keep in mind when you are writing supporting statements or letters of application that this is your greatest pre-interview opportunity to shine. Don't waste it!
- Never attempt to craft a statement that you can bend to fit all the applications that you make. Each application needs its own unique statement. (OK, you're bound to borrow choice phrases or paragraphs from previous statements that you have written, but that's where the similarity should end – the last thing heads and governors want to see is a statement that applies to a job in another school; they get understandably touchy about these things!)
- Repeat as a mantra: I must match my unique selling skills to the job description and person specification. Never forget that most crucial point.
- Back your experiences up with examples showing evidence of your *skills* and *achievements*.
- Optimise the positive! It's amazing how many supporting statements I've read that simply don't *sell* the writer. They can be bland and uninspired and some even apologetically mention negative points such as: 'I'm not very good at organising my time but I hope to improve in the future'! That's going to get chucked out immediately by any head needing you to hit the ground running in your new job.
- Begin and end your statement with real impact. You'll know when you've got it right!

- Don't be shy about conveying a sense of your personality. That's what's going to hit the reader and create a longing to find out more in an interview.
- Include a sentence about what motivates you to teach.
- Make sure that your grammar is impeccable throughout. Every spelling error or grammatical mistake *will* be picked up by heads and governors, who are looking for as close to perfection as they can get. You owe it to yourself to ensure that your entire application is error free.
- Keep it concise and use 'action' words. Edit your first draft right down to create space to include even more examples of your skills and achievements just to make sure that every point in the job description and person specification is covered.
- If possible, get someone to read through your statement to check for errors and potentially clumsy sentence construction. Don't be proud at this stage; every piece of written work can benefit from sensitive editing!

I need ideas for my supporting statement. Where can I find examples to read?

This is the worst thing you can do! Don't whatever you do take ideas from someone else's statement or from some of the examples it's possible to find online. I know it sounds tough, but the only way your statement is going to sell *you* is if it is written in *your* words and it matches, specifically, the person specification for a particular job. It is easy for heads and governors to spot statements that have been rehashed from examples when they are shortlisting; they lack energy and enthusiasm and invariably fail to connect specifically to what the school is actually searching for. If you write without relying on examples from other people or for mythical jobs, you have a far greater chance of getting *your* suitability for the job across.

Who should I put down as a referee?

Often schools and local education authorities are specific about who they want you to put down as a referee. Usually this will be someone who knows you as a person or in a professional capacity and someone who can comment on your work as a teacher. Think carefully about who you will choose, as a poor or indifferent reference can be enough to put a head off making an appointment. Make sure that whoever you select is in a position to match your qualities to what the job requires and always ask their permission first before adding them to an application form. You want them to be in as good a mood as possible when they sit down to write your reference!

I suspect that one of my references isn't as good as it might be. Is there anything I can do about that?

You can make a request to see your references by contacting the data controller in the school you *apply* to. Data protection regulations aren't concerned as much with confidentiality as they are with the factual accuracy of what is written about people. But remember, ask the school *receiving* your reference, not the individual *writing* it.

If, when you have read your reference, you think that it isn't as fair as it could be, it would be wise to contact your union for advice on how to take your particular situation forward to a positive solution. You don't have to accept an unfair reference, but the more evidence you can provide showing the inaccuracies it contains, the better.

You can find out more about your right to see your references from the Information Commissioner's Office:
www.informationcommissioner.gov.uk.

I've heard that some LEAs operate a pool system. What is this?

This means that LEAs invite applications from those who know they want to work in the area. The applications are to join a pool of new teachers that schools in the area can draw from. They are not applications for specific jobs in specific schools. Being accepted into a pool in an LEA does not necessarily mean that you will get a job in the area, but it does mean that your pool application will be forwarded to schools in some way (increasingly electronically) as and when vacancies arise. It is still worth keeping a close eye out for any vacancies that are advertised within the area and outside. Don't rely on acceptance into a pool providing you with a job, but it is definitely worth applying to pools, as it does make sure that you have as many bases covered as possible. This type of pool system is different from the supply pools that LEAs operate or have operated for them.

I trained in Wales but want to teach in England. Can I do that?

Yes you can, and vice versa too, under mutual recognition of qualifications arrangements.

I go to pieces at interviews. How can I keep the nerves to a minimum?

If you're fortunate enough to get an offer of an interview after all the hard work of applying, the last thing you want to do is scupper your chances by letting nerves take over. The best way to shine through during an interview is to *enjoy* it! And if you can't muster any degree of enjoyment from the situation, at least act as if you can!

There are many things that you can do to calm your nerves. You may want to talk to your GP about what he or she can offer you but personally I'm not a huge advocate of pill popping unless absolutely essential. You'll probably feel calmer and clearer headed if you take the following measures before an interview:

- Get plenty of sleep so that you're not stressed simply through tiredness.
- Eat balanced meals the day before (well, every day, but particularly the day before an interview) and a healthy, energy-giving breakfast the morning of an interview.
- Be mindful of the way in which you're thinking about the interview. Turn negative, self-defeating thoughts into positive ones: there is every chance that you'll get this job!
- When you feel yourself starting to panic, calm your nerves through slow, rhythmic breathing.

- There are many harmless natural solutions to nervousness out there. Many swear by the impact of Bach Rescue Remedy but there are other brands to explore too. A good natural health store will be able to help you find something that's right for you.
- If nerves become a major issue for you, it would be worth considering addressing them specifically with a qualified practitioner. Homeopathy, reflexology, neuro-linguistic programming and aromatherapy are just some of the therapies on offer with good track records in helping to quell nerves.

It may be easier said than done, but really, there's no need to fear interviews. They are a necessary stage in the job hunting process and the more comfortable you can become with the idea of talking about yourself and your work, the better your chances of success will be.

> If nerves really do seem to get out of control and prevent you from moving forward in your life, it really is important to seek the help of a trained health care provider.

What questions am I likely to be asked during an interview?

It's impossible to say! And in reality, it's probably best that you don't know in advance otherwise you'd be so aware of delivering a scripted answer that all your spontaneity, passion and enthusiasm would be squeezed out of you. However, there are likely topics to be covered, as follows:

- You may be asked to talk about your experiences in the profession so far, whether that's as a trainee or a supply teacher.
- Interviewers will probably want to know how you would deal with certain 'problem' scenarios, for example, an irate parent or a persistently disruptive child.

- Questions regarding assessment, and how you know your assessment of a child is accurate are bound to come up.
- You'll probably be asked in some way about your ability to work as part of a team and your ability to work independently when necessary.
- Your accomplishments and career aspirations will feature at some point.
- Strengths and development needs may be covered.
- You may be asked to talk about additional subjects and skills that you could bring to the school.
- Your abilities to handle the demands of the job and maintain a work–life balance could be covered.

This isn't in any way an exhaustive list, but you may like to think about how you would address these issues.

It's fine to take a moment to consider how you want to answer a question. A considered response is far better than one which tumbles out, never quite hitting the key point of the question, then tails off in a vague confusion! Listen carefully to each question as it is asked, and don't be afraid to ask for clarity or for it to be repeated if necessary. Then focus your response directly on the question asked, calmly and with a quiet confidence.

If I'm asked if I have any questions at the end of an interview, what if I can't think of any? Will that look bad?

Don't worry at all if you don't have any questions to ask but make sure that you say something like 'All the questions I had have been covered, thank you'. That said, it's a good idea to keep some general questions up your sleeve as well as making a mental note of anything that you can ask about or comment on that arises throughout the course of the interview process. You might like to ask questions along the following themes:

- What would be the arrangements for my induction period?
- Would I have a tutor group?
- Would I have to teach personal, social and health education?
- Would I be able to offer an extra-curricular activity?
- How active is the parent staff association?
- How involved are the governors at this school?
- Does the school organise any school journeys or day trips?

The list of possible questions is endless but similarly, it's quite possible that all outstanding questions are covered during the interview. As long as you make it sound as though you did have questions but that they have all been covered, it's fine not to ask any.

The letter I received inviting me for an interview says that I can take a portfolio along if I wish. What should I include in it?

Portfolios are an excellent way of demonstrating your skills, experiences and achievements in a tangible and visual way. As a governor I love to look through portfolios when I'm on interview panels as they offer so much additional information about a candidate.

Although it's not essential to have a portfolio, there is now an expectation that NQTs will have one and it's worth spending some time getting yours just right. Ideally, use an A3 folder (unless you have a lot of larger pieces of art work to include) think about how you will present the contents (for example, what style of labelling you will use and so on). Be consistent throughout. The following pointers on contents will help, although this is not intended to be an exhaustive list:

- Samples of various types of planning, for example, short term and medium term.
- Some lesson plans.
- Photographs of children's work or special displays or events you have been involved in.
- Examples of your assessment of children's work.

- Something that shows your knowledge of current priorities in education (for example 'Excellence and Enjoyment' in the primary sector).
- Examples that indicate your knowledge of the importance of cross-curricular dimensions of the curriculum such as ICT, literacy and emotional development.
- You may also like to include a brief summary (a sentence or two) outlining your philosophy of education.

Aim to create a pool of items you can include in your portfolio so that you refresh it for each interview you attend throughout your career. Just like your supporting statement, the closer your portfolio can be to demonstrating the skills that the school is actually looking for the better.

Help! I've got a job

I'm going to be starting a new job in a new area and I have no idea how to find decent accommodation in time for the start of the school year. What should I do?

First port of call should be the LEA's teaching personnel office (some have fancy names for this but they basically amount to the same thing). They will be able to give you contact details of reputable rental companies in the area and the LEA may even have some properties specifically for the use of new teachers (some still do, although not that many now). Do also ask if they have a list of people who are willing to rent out rooms to teachers in the area. Although being a lodger may not be your ideal, it would at least give you an opportunity to get to know the area before making a decision on where you want to live. Don't forget that the internet can be a great way of finding out about new places too. There are many websites out there to help you find rental accommodation and information about the facilities nearby: www.fish4.co.uk is a good place to start.

If you are considering purchasing a property, you may be eligible for help under various schemes run by the Office of the Deputy Prime Minister (ODPM).

> The Office of the Deputy Prime Minister website can be found here: www.odpm.gov.uk. Alternatively you can call the enquiry line: 020 7944 4400.

I'm going to be starting my new job in September but should I go into school beforehand?

This is entirely up to you. However, there's no doubt that if you have the opportunity to go into school and at least get your classroom sorted out and organised as you would like it to be, the start of the new term will be smoother for you. It would be a good idea to talk to your head teacher about the times when you could have access to your classroom before the term starts and then make a decision over how much time you'd like to devote to it.

You may also like to consider going into school to observe any children currently there who you will be teaching in September. This can be a great way of starting to get to know names and likes and dislikes etc.

> Any time spent in school in advance of your job starting is a bonus. You are not obliged to do this but will almost certainly benefit from any school visits you can make.

I've got a new job but haven't got a contract yet. Should I be sent one before the start of term?

In an ideal world you would receive a written contract to sign before actually starting your new job but in reality this rarely happens. There isn't a sinister reason behind this – it's purely an administrative thing. As long as you have written confirmation of your job offer and as many details connected to the job as possible (who you will be teaching, the subjects you will be teaching and your time-table, your salary and so on) it doesn't matter too much if the contract isn't in your hands for the first day of term. That said, don't let things slide for weeks before asking for a contract. It can sometimes take a little while for LEAs or governors to get contracts out to new staff but certainly don't let it go on longer than the first two weeks of term, which is a reasonable amount of time to wait.

> If you have any concerns whatsoever about the terms and conditions of your employment, get in touch with your union.

I'm starting work in a few months but haven't yet got round to joining a union. Is it really necessary?

Yes. There is no doubt about this. I can't tell you which union to join (union membership is covered in more detail in Chapter 9) but it is really important that you give yourself the kind of protection that union membership offers, professional insurance being the main example. Unions also offer all sorts of other member benefits as well as being an important conduit of information between teachers in the profession and the policy makers and politicians in the Department for Education and Skills. If you are considering not being a member of a union, you will need to consider where you will get the kind of cover and protection that unions offer their members.

> Teachers often say that they joined a particular union because that's what the majority of teachers in their school belonged to. This makes no difference whatsoever. It's essential that you join the union that best meets your needs as a teacher. Don't even consider what union other teachers in your school belong to. Make your own choice based on your needs.

CHAPTER 2

Making a start

The only way to deal with the future is to function efficiently in the Now.

(Gita Bellin)

Introduction

After the exertions of initial teacher training, and the sometimes challenging process of finding a job to apply for, actually making the application and going through the demands of an interview, it can be easy to sit back in satisfaction without a thought for what it will be like on your first day. While I would never suggest doing so much preparation that you hit the ground at an exhausted plod rather than a comfortably enthusiastic pace, it is well worth putting some effort into ensuring that your entry to the profession is as smooth as possible.

Making a seamless transition from training to employment (or, if you have taken an employment-based route into teaching, from training to full qualification) is significantly important. This time can help to set your attitude and approach to your career, and can impact your levels of present and future enjoyment of it. A good start counts for a lot!

This chapter looks at the questions that typically arise when new teachers take their first steps in the career with qualified teacher status.

FAQs in this chapter cover:

- Preparing to start your new job
- Induction tutor concerns
- Being a tutor
- Meeting a class before the start of term
- Setting your room up
- Career Entry and Development Profile (CEDP)
- First aid
- Assemblies
- Ofsted inspection
- Home tutoring

Preparing to start your new job

I can't wait to get started with my new job and my own class for the first time, but what should I be doing in the summer holiday to make sure my first term kicks off well?

Ultimately, you should be relaxing! Take advantage of this holiday so that you start the term refreshed, energised and ready to go. That said, you will feel more confident about the start of term if you have organised your classroom and planned your first week at least. It's a good idea to ask for all the schemes of work that you'll be needing as well as class lists and any relevant policies and handbooks you'll need to be familiar with. Consider how you want your room arranged (although do find out if there are any rules and regulations you need to stick to) and think about what displays you want on the walls. It's always good for your pupils to see their own work displayed but this won't be possible until you've had a chance to work with them first. In the mean time, posters and artefacts relating to the themes you'll be teaching first of all can make inspirational and interactive displays that the children can enjoy. In short, do what will take the edge off any concerns you have about the start of term, but don't work so hard that you end up jaded before you even hit the mid-point of September. Part of your success as an NQT will be to do with how well you can pace yourself through each term, so use the long summer break to build up your reserves and ensure that you're ready to go on the first day of term!

I don't seem to have been given an induction tutor. Does that matter?

Yes it does. You should have been assigned someone who can oversee your induction and be responsible for ensuring that the induction that you receive is targeted and specific to the needs you have discussed between you. Induction is all about your transition from training to employment and your early professional development and it's essential to have a single person responsible for bringing this together. The first step to take is to talk to your head teacher. If your school is a small one it may be that your induction tutor is actually your head teacher, but in any event, this should be made clear to you. If you are still unsure about who your induction tutor is after talking to your head teacher, you should discuss the situation with the person responsible for NQTs within your local education authority. This person should know all about the induction arrangements for all the NQTs in the LEA. Whatever you do, don't continue without finding out exactly who your induction tutor is.

I've been told that I'll be having a tutor group when I start my new job. I thought that NQTs weren't supposed to have tutor groups. Is there anything I can do about it?

There's nothing in the induction guidance to say that NQTs shouldn't have tutor groups. In fact, I'd go as far as to say that it's a positive advantage to have a tutor group and that those who don't have one are missing out on a really significant aspect of school life.

While your school is within its rights to ask you to be a tutor, and you wouldn't be wise, in my opinion, to ask to be excused this role, it would be perfectly reasonable to ask for guidance on successfully running a tutor group. It could be that this becomes a focus on your Career Entry and Development Profile and there may be a local or online course you can do to improve your skills and confidence.

It's highly likely that once you get into being a tutor, you'll really start to enjoy the role and use it to build effective working relationships with all your students.

You can find out more about this element of pastoral care in schools from the National Association for Pastoral Care in Education (NAPCE): www.napce.org.uk.

I didn't have much chance to work with a tutor when I was training and now I'm going to be one! What does the role entail?

It's extremely difficult to define precisely what the role of a tutor entails, partly because this can vary from school to school and partly because it can be seemingly limitless!

The Newly Qualified Teacher's Handbook identifies the following aspects of the role of tutor:

- inspirer/morale booster
- listener
- counsellor
- communicator
- problem solver
- administrator
- nurturer
- enabler
- monitor of academic progress
- monitor of social development
- manager of behaviour
- praise giver
- motivator
- team builder
- confidant

When you start your new job, be sure to ask what is expected of tutors in your school. If you are in a year group or in a house system there are likely to be other more experienced tutors who can support you through your first term as a tutor and beyond. Draw on their advice and ideas, but also, don't be afraid to develop your own thoughts on how you want to operate as a tutor (within any guidelines laid down by your school). For you to feel happy in the role, you'll need to be working in a way that suits your personality. Feel free to expand the role as you see fit so as to ensure that your tutees' experience of school is as humane and supportive of their development as young adults as possible.

> There is more information on the role of the tutor in *The Newly Qualified Teacher's Handbook* www.nqthandbook.info. Always be guided by your school's requirements of its tutors.

I'm going to be meeting my new class before the end of the summer term. Have you got any tips on what I should aim to do with them?

This depends very much on the age of the children and the amount of time that you have with each other but there are some generic ideas to consider:

- You want the first meeting to be light and amicable, but at the same time, remember that for all of us, however old we are, first impressions count.
- Introduce yourself as you want to be known and do an activity based on getting to know certain aspects of the group as a whole and as individuals, including something simple around learning names (although be aware that depending on their age, they may well change quite significantly over the summer break!).
- Aim to find some common ground with the group (is there something you all enjoy?) and build on that. Use plenty of positive

reinforcement and express how much you're going to enjoy teaching them. Pick out something to praise the whole group for (for example, 'I'm going to love teaching you next year – you're all such great listeners! We're going to get on really well together'). That way you're almost programming success!

- Use the opportunity to ask them what they *want* you to know about them. Also make sure that you take the opportunity to find out from other teachers what you *ought* to know!
- Get the group to focus on one thing that they're looking forward to in the next year at school, and one thing they are apprehensive about. You can do this through an activity or a discussion, depending on their age. Keep a record of these hopes and fears and revisit them when you start your new job.

> For more specific advice for the age group or subject that you will be teaching, you could pose a question in an online teacher staffroom such as that found at www.eteach.com.

I'm really excited about having my own classroom at last. What do I need to consider when I set it up for the new term?

It's great to have your own domain in which to set all your systems up and get things ready for the new term. It is worth considering what kind of environment you want to create, and these points may help:

- Aim at least to start off the term clutter-free. It can quickly build up over time!
- Zone your teaching space so that it is clear to all who use it what each area is for. While this sounds more applicable for the primary classroom, it also works in the secondary classroom where you may want to establish certain areas where lesson resources can be collected from or where homework can be left and marked books retrieved.

- Think about how you want to decorate your room. It's always important to use your pupils' work, but you may also want to use stimulus material linked to topics you'll be covering such as posters and artefacts. Plants can be good in a classroom too.
- Consider how you will keep the air quality as high as possible. Simply keeping windows open for fresh air can help.
- Make sure the heating system can be controlled. You don't want any extremes of temperature or nothing will get done in your room!
- Keep everything tidy and organised for maximum safety.
- Think about how you might use colour and sound to create an atmosphere conducive to learning.
- Experiment with different seating arrangements.
- If applicable, think about any names you'll be giving clusters of tables – will you use a theme such as authors or planets, or will you give your pupils the choice?
- Where will you mainly be functioning from? Can every child see you? Hear you?

I haven't been told much about the Career Entry and Development Profile. What is it?

The Career Entry and Development Profile is a collection of online materials (although hard copies are available from your initial teacher training provider) that have been designed specifically to help trainees and NQTs to think about their professional development as a teacher. It is used at key points towards the end of your teacher training and during induction.

Basically, the intention is for NQTs to make connections between their training and their induction. It will help you to focus on your achievements to date as well as your goals for the future and this process should support your development as a reflective practitioner in the classroom.

I'd rather not use the CEDP during my induction. Is that OK?

No! There's no choice, you have to use it. That's a good thing though, as it is thought to be a really effective way of NQTs and induction tutors sharing and revising ideas about the induction plan that NQTs follow.

Is the induction plan the same as the CEDP?

No it isn't. The CEDP is designed to support the induction planning process as it helps NQTs to gather evidence and become more reflective about their work. Your induction action plan will set out clear objectives for your targeted induction; one can inform the other.

What are the three transition points of the CEDP?

The three transition points occur at the following times:

- towards the end of your initial teacher training
- when you start your induction
- when you complete your induction.

Do I have to do anything in particular at these transition points?

Yes you do. There is guidance in the CEDP for each of the transition points as well as a collection of questions that have been devised to prompt your thinking and help inform your discussions with your induction tutor. There are also supplementary support materials which you may find useful.

The Training and Development Agency for Schools (TDA) suggests the following points for each transition point.

Transition point 1

This section will help you to think about your experiences before, during and outside your initial teacher training programme. It can help you to identify your key achievements and aspirations as a teacher. The TDA suggests that NQTs will also want to think about where professional development should concentrate in order to

- reflect and build on the strengths in your practice
- develop aspects of the teacher's role in which you are particularly interested
- provide more experience, or build up your expertise, in areas where you have developed to a more limited extent so far.

Transition point 2

This is the point at which you and your induction tutor plan your induction support programme (this is an important stage and part of the induction arrangements for NQTs which are statutory). You should discuss your priorities for development as they stand *now* so that your induction can begin to focus on these needs right from the start. Possibly the most important aspect of this stage is the *process* of reflection and discussion that you and your induction tutor go through.

The TDA suggests that, at this point, NQTs will be able to draw on the evidence they have, for example:

- the notes you made at transition point 1 and the evidence and reasoning underlying them
- the information you have been given about the school and your role
- the output from any additional experience or development you have gained between being awarded qualified teacher status and starting your induction period.

Transition point 3

This is the point at which you can reflect back on your induction period and on your progress so far, the induction support programme that you are so close to completing, and your hopes and aspirations for the next stages of your continuing professional development (CPD) in your career. This is very much a period of reviewing and 'taking stock' of everything you have faced as an NQT, and just how far you have come. The discussions that you have at this stage are very important as they will help you to look forward to your continuing success in the profession.

The TDA suggests that the discussions you have at transition point 3 are likely to

- reflect on your own learning as a teacher
- identify the conditions and circumstances which enable you to develop as a teacher
- focus on your CPD needs for your second year of teaching, and
- prepare for involvement in the school's performance management arrangements.

> There is extensive advice and guidance on the CEDP on the Training and Development Agency for Schools website: www.tda.gov.uk.

I've never had any first aid training but feel as though I should now that I'm going to be in charge of my classes alone. Is it necessary?

You may go through your entire career without ever needing to use skills of first aid. However, you may be faced with children having their first epileptic fit in your classroom or their first asthma attack, not to mention children with known pre-existing health conditions that could affect them at school, and knowing what to do to help them could make a dramatic difference.

Always talk to your head teacher or induction tutor about any concerns you have about your ability and appropriateness to administer first aid. It is important that you understand who, in your school, is a qualified first aider, and exactly what would be expected of you in a situation in which first aid is necessary.

There is extensive advice on first aid in *The Newly Qualified Teacher's Handbook*: www.nqthandbook.info. You can also find out about first aid courses from the British Red Cross First Aid Training website: www.redcrossfirstaidtraining.co.uk or from the St John Ambulance website: www.sja.org.uk/.

I know that I'm going to have to take an assembly with my class because all the teachers take it in turns, but I've never had to do that before. Where can I find ideas?

Even a quick search on an internet search engine will come up with countless websites with assembly ideas. Your school may have a favourite source of ideas too, so it would be worth asking your colleagues. Do also find out the extent of religious input there should be in each assembly. Collective worship in schools should be 'wholly or mainly of a broadly Christian character' but secular assemblies can be held in schools too. Your head teacher will be able to explain your school's policy on this.

Don't forget that assemblies can be a fantastic opportunity to nurture your students' spiritual, moral, social and cultural development too, as well as a chance to focus on citizenship issues. Many charities have assembly ideas too, which promote their particular interests in the world.

These websites are good places to start searching for assembly ideas:

- Amnesty International UK: www.amnesty.org.uk
- British Humanist Association: www.humanism.org.uk
- Save the Children: www.oneworld.org
- Society for the Promotion of Christian Knowledge: www.assemblies.org

continued on next page

Do also look out for campaigns run by charities such as Comic Relief (which runs Red Nose Day and Sport Relief) as their websites will have assemblies and other teacher resources that can be downloaded and easily put to use. The weekly newsletter that www.eteach.com sends to registered users often carries news of such charity campaigns and free lesson resources in its 'lowdown' feature.

I'm about to start my new job and I don't know what I'm supposed to wear. Do all schools have a dress code?

If you're ever in doubt, dress in a smartly comfortable way. Your clothes have got to be practical for teaching but can also be smart. Once you have been at the school for a while you'll get a feel for what is acceptable and what teachers typically wear there.

Most schools do have a dress code or at least some guidance for teachers on what is expected. It's also perfectly acceptable to ask about the dress code if you are uncertain.

I've been told that my school is likely to be inspected during my first year there. I'm starting to panic already! Where can I find out more about inspection?

Whatever you do, don't panic! Inspection is a part of life as a teacher and they are not necessarily stressful events. Think of it as your chance to show what a great teacher you are!

Inspection is not all about endless preparation and paperwork. It is about finding out how your school is functioning, how well the children are learning and the teachers are teaching, and what progress it has made since the last time it was inspected, among other things. It is an essential part of the accountability process and can really help schools to focus on their ongoing self-evaluations. At the end of an inspection you will know exactly what it is that your school does well, what it needs to focus on and what its goals for the future might include.

The Office for Standards in Education (Ofsted) manages the system of inspection in England (Wales, Northern Ireland and Scotland have their own equivalents) and you can find out all you need to know from: www.ofsted.gov.uk.

I'd like to do some home tutoring to supplement my income. Can I do this in my NQT year?

Yes you can, there's nothing to stop you, but it's a good idea to think carefully about whether you have the time to do this. If you do decide that you can fit it in, the following ideas may help:

- Think about what subjects or skills you are willing to offer lessons in. Don't feel restricted to what is offered in schools. Think laterally to increase your potential field of clients.
- Work out what you want to charge each hour and decide whether you are willing to offer discounts for teaching small groups or for clients who pay for, say, ten lessons all at once.
- Decide *where* you will teach. Do you want people to come to your home or will you go to theirs? Be sure to think through any safety implications (the Suzy Lamplugh Trust website carries a huge amount of very useful advice on personal safety: www.suzylamplugh.org).
- Think about how long each lesson will be and how many lessons you want to teach each week.
- It is a good idea always to offer for a child's parent or carer to sit in on the lessons. If possible, avoid the situation where you will be alone with a child.
- Think about how you will get clients. Some home tutors accept new children only through word of mouth while others put an advert in the local paper.

CHAPTER 3

Working on supply

Until you try, you don't know what you can't do.

(Henry James)

Introduction

Not every new teacher gets a permanent job for the start of the academic year following qualification. For some, the flexibility that supply teaching offers is just what they need to broaden their experience and allow them time to gain confidence before launching their careers with a full-time permanent position. For others, there just hasn't been the right job to go for or they haven't been successful in their quest for employment so far.

Supply teaching can offer teachers many benefits, whatever stage of their career they are at. OK, it's not always ideal for NQTs, but it needn't be a disaster and is a certain way to find out a huge amount very quickly about yourself and who you are as a teacher. Supply teaching helps teachers to gain confidence in their ability to think on their feet, to adapt to the changing circumstances around them, to assess the mood of a class in a moment, to find out about a range of schools in an area and to gather vital skills such as classroom management and time management. This is all incredibly valuable stuff, not to be dismissed!

Whatever circumstances have led you to this point, if you are looking down the barrel of supply work as your route into paid teaching, there are certain issues to be aware of. The following questions typically arise from NQTs who are about to embark on supply teaching at this stage of their careers.

FAQs in this chapter cover:

- Short-term supply teaching
- Eligibility to teach on supply
- Getting supply work
- Supply and the four-term rule
- Employability after supply teaching
- Supply teaching nerves
- Behaviour management
- Being a good supply teacher
- Turning supply teaching down
- Supply and the General Teaching Council
- Long-term supply
- Induction and supply
- Covering maternity leave

Short-term supply

If I don't get a permanent job can I do supply teaching?

Yes you can but there are, at the time of writing, certain restrictions attached. If the supply teaching is short term, i.e. day-to-day or even week-to-week supply (which is common in schools that just need to cover the short-term absences of staff) then you can do this only for four terms. The clock starts ticking from the date of your first short-term placement after gaining qualified teacher status and are measured as a fixed calendar period rather than an aggregate total of supply completed. That means that if you qualify in, say, August, and you do one day of supply in the whole of the following autumn term, you have effectively used up one whole term of your four-term limit. If you then do nothing for the following spring term and a handful of days in the summer term you will have used up three terms of your four-term limit. Get it? If you reach the end of your four-term limit without managing to get inductable work (there's loads more on this in Chapter 4), you cannot continue to do supply work, unless you go for an extension.

How do I go about getting supply work?

There are three main ways of getting supply work:

- Join an LEA supply pool – get in touch with any LEAs you would like to supply in and find out what the procedures are for joining the pool. Alternatively visit www.supplypool.co.uk.
- Join a supply agency – there are several of these, details of which can be found online or in your local Yellow Pages.
- Write to schools direct – send in your CV and a covering letter stating that you are available for supply work. This is more likely to work if you already have connections with the school in question.

Regardless of how you go about getting supply work you should ensure that you will have at least the following:

- pay based on your experience and qualifications
- pension rights through the teacher's pension scheme (TPS)
- access to LEA grievance and disciplinary procedures.

The more loyalty you can show a school or supply pool, the more likely you are to be called for regular work. Aim to approach supply work as professionally as possible and the chances are you'll have plenty to do!

Is there a standard rate of pay for supply teachers?

No, there isn't. If you're working for a private agency they are free to pay you whatever they want to pay you (or rather, whatever they have agreed to pay you). However, if you work through an LEA you must be paid in accordance with the pay arrangements for teachers that are laid out in the School Teachers' Pay and Conditions Document. This means that as a supply teacher you should be paid on a daily basis (using the assumption that a year constitutes 195 days).

> There is more information on this on Teachernet: www.teachernet. gov.uk/pay.

I am at the end of my four-term limit and still don't have an inductable post. What now?

If you're at, or nearing, the end of the limit, you can ask your LEA for an extension to the four-term rule. LEAs have the right to extend new teachers' entitlements to work on short-term supply jobs in 'exceptional circumstances'. These are:

- being unable to find inductable work due to a shortage of jobs in your area
- personal circumstances such as childcare issues or other care commitments that mean that you cannot move to where jobs may be
- serious illness meaning that you are unable to take on a post of a term or more in duration.

LEAs grant extensions on a case-by-case basis but I've yet to hear of a request that has been refused. The extension can be for no more than twelve months and you should receive written confirmation that the limit has been extended with start and end dates. It's important to realise that this extension would apply only to schools in that LEA. You'd need to go through the process again if you wanted to change LEAs or work across more than one.

Who keeps track of the four-term supply rule?

Interesting question! The short answer is that you do. You know that the rule exists and it's up to you to abide by it. It would be easy enough for an LEA, the GTC or a school to work out if you had gone over the limit so it makes sense to keep track for yourself and if it looks like you may go over, request an extension sooner rather than later. Don't just let things slide hoping that no one will notice. Keep on top of it and you won't be criticised.

I haven't got a job and feel like I'm a failure doing day-to-day supply when I can get it. Will a school ever want to employ me?

When you feel like this at any point of your career, it's time to sit down and write out all the positive skills you have acquired since starting your supply work. There's no doubt that having experience of what it's like in different schools will definitely help you to work out what kind of environment is right for you as well as giving you the chance to see how a wide range of teachers work. You also have the opportunity to try out different techniques in relatively highly pressured circumstances and to adapt the way you work to suit the needs of those in front of you. These are invaluable experiences and skills to acquire and they offer you many positive benefits. Your task is to make sure that you put all that across in any applications that you make. Always emphasise the positive (don't say 'I'm only doing supply because I haven't got a job', say 'Working as a supply teacher has been the best decision I ever made as far as my personal and professional development is concerned' – see the difference?), relate your learning to your classroom practice and sell your skills. Why would a school *not* want to employ you?

I've got my first supply job booked and I'm really nervous. Are there any top tips I should keep in mind?

It's only natural to feel nervous about your first supply job. It's a big thing to do and can be very daunting. It's great that you're not letting your nerves stop you from taking the plunge though! There is an endless number of tips for supply teachers but here are the ones you'll probably find most useful:

- Gather together some basic resources that you can use should you find that no work has been set. Some supply teachers find that their 'supply kit' grows over time to include basic lesson plans, pens and pencils, paper, trainers (in case of needing to do a PE lesson), worksheets, time-filling activities, tissues and so on. There are plenty of online resources for supply teachers to be found at: www.supplypool.co.uk.

- Keep a supply notebook in which you can jot down any innovative ideas you come across in the schools you visit. Nothing wrong with being a magpie!

- There is an enormous amount of online resources for teachers which can be downloaded onto a laptop, if you have one, and plundered and printed if necessary when you get to a school. Check out all the resources on www.teachernet.gov.uk and www.supplypool.co.uk for starters.

- Always introduce yourself to the class. You may like to say that you're not new to the school but are new to that class.

- Ask a couple of friendly looking students to help you out with learning names. Some supply teachers ask children to write their names on a sticker that they wear for the lesson or day.

- Take some tea or coffee money in with you in case you're asked to make a contribution for any drinks you have (not all schools will ask but some may). Some experienced supply teachers take their own mugs in just in case.

I'm terrified about how I'm going to control the classes on my first day of supply. Any tips and ideas?

This is a very common concern for new teachers embarking on supply work. It can be incredibly daunting to face new children in an unfamiliar school and know that you have to take them through the day or lesson as smoothly and effectively as possible.

The following ideas will help you to keep cool and calm in the face of potential disruption:

- Find out as much as you can about the class or classes beforehand. Get a class list and mark any relevant information (perhaps in a code only you will understand) against each name.

- Make sure that you are familiar with the school's discipline or behaviour policy and don't be afraid to refer to it.
- Go in with the expectation that the students will listen and respond positively to you; be aware of your classroom presence – make it felt in an authoritative, firm yet open way.
- Spend a brief moment talking about your expectations of them and theirs of you.
- Appeal to their better natures! This does work, especially if you need to quell a situation that involves just a few.
- Act sooner rather than later in the event of minor indiscipline – intervene with calm words and assertive body language as early as possible to prevent situations from escalating.
- Don't be afraid to lean on the support of other teachers. This will show that you mean business, and undoubtedly the more you are in a particular school, the less you will have to do this. If you are having specific difficulties with a class or a student, aim to talk to other teachers during break or lunchtime to gain insights into how best to handle them.
- Be careful about dishing out your own sanctions that aren't part of the school's discipline or behaviour policy. Always check that what you intend to do is acceptable and remember that you will be expected to carry out your own pupil sanctions. Any sanctions that you issue must be followed up (don't issue idle threats – that's the quickest way to diminish respect) and remember to report back to the class teacher any sanctions you have had to dish out.

I haven't been told anything about how to be a good supply teacher. What do I need to know?

Much of what you need to know you would probably do instinctively anyway. Basically, you need to turn up in good time, show willing and aim to leave the place better than you found it! In reality this might mean doing any of the following, particularly if you want to be called back for more work:

- If you know in advance which classes you will be taking or which subjects you'll be covering, you may be able to do some preparation beforehand. Always ask in advance if work will be set and aim to get as much information as you can about what is expected of you.
- Arrive as early as you can on the morning of your first day of supply in a school so that you can gather all the necessary resources you need and prepare yourself for the day.
- Attend the pre-school briefing if there is one.
- Ask to be introduced to key members of staff such as the head of department or key stage coordinator. There should be someone you can call on if you need assistance.
- Be aware that you may have tutoring duties as well as teaching duties. Find out how registration is done in the school (by hand or electronically) and whether you will have any responsibilities for it.
- Be aware that you should, unless told otherwise, do as much marking or assessment of the work you have done with each class as possible. It's also a good idea to initial the work and indicate that you marked it as a supply teacher.
- You may be asked to perform break time supervision.
- Always return any resources you have borrowed and make sure any rooms you use are left tidy by the classes you cover.
- Leave a brief run-down of the day or each lesson for the relevant teachers on their return. Note the work covered, how it was received by the students, any problems encountered and so on.
- Let someone know when you leave, preferably the head if possible. If you can provide some positive feedback about how well the day has gone, this is likely to be remembered the next time the school needs supply cover (assuming, of course, that you would want to return!).

The teacher recruitment website www.eteach.com, which also facilitates supply pools for many of the UK's LEAs (www.supplypool.co.uk), carries a very useful code of practice for supply teachers:

- Always arrive punctually – inform the school immediately of any travel delays.
- Maintain professional standards of dress and appropriate behaviour while in schools.
- Keep up-to-date on National Curriculum issues and your subject specialisms.
- Teach and supervise classes effectively, to the best of your ability.
- Prepare lessons when known, or teach the lessons provided by the school as appropriate.
- Provide your own materials and classroom resources so that you are able to 'stand alone' in emergency bookings.
- For advance bookings, where information is available, make the necessary preparations to deliver relevant lessons to your classes.
- Mark any written work by primary classes before leaving at the end of each day.
- Mark the written work that you have set in secondary schools, where applicable.
- Leave notes for permanent teachers where appropriate.
- Carry out reasonable requests made by the head or supervising teacher, including tasks like playground or lunch duty etc.
- Contact Eteach's helpdesk immediately should you have any problems.

If you decide to join an LEA supply pool facilitated by Eteach.com, you will be asked to follow these points for best practice. This helps to give a clear idea of what is expected of a supply teacher working within an LEA supply pool.

Members of the pool will:

- Register and maintain their own personal and teaching details on the service provider's website.
- Keep an up-to-date online diary as provided by Eteach.
- By registering, agree to the service provider's agency agreement.
- Provide information required in order to meet the criteria for registration, contact and payroll.

- Respond quickly to requests for confirmation of availability.
- Advise the school provider immediately if unable to honour a commitment to an assignment.
- Arrive at the school at the prearranged time and report to the school contact.
- Have relevant and appropriate materials available for use on emergency bookings.
- Teach lessons prepared by class teacher as appropriate.
- Maintain a professional standard of dress when attending schools.
- Leave the classroom as they would expect to find it.
- Advise the service provider of any complaints/grievances.
- Conduct themselves appropriately as professional supply teachers in the school.
- Familiarise themselves with individual school policy and procedure by reviewing the school information held on the Eteach website.
- Familiarise themselves with LEA policies including contact with children, health and safety and grievance procedures.

I've been asked to go back to a school to do some supply but I absolutely hated it when I was there. How can I get out of it but still get asked to do supply in other schools?

It may be an idea to hold back from saying how much you hated the school and simply decline the offer of work by saying that you have been booked elsewhere and leave it at that. If you are working closely with a supply pool or agency then honesty is usually the best policy. Not all schools will suit every teacher and if you mention that it would be your preference to work elsewhere before returning to a particular school, most supply pool or agency staff will understand what you mean. As long as you aim to get the outcome you desire without burning any bridges, you will be keeping as many options open as you can and will be thought of as a professional, who is committed to your supply work, rather than someone who is simply filling in time between jobs or before getting a job.

If I only do a very small amount of supply teaching do I still need to be registered with the GTC?

Yes you do, and this is a legal requirement if you want to do any amount of supply (even just an hour!) in a maintained school, a non-maintained special school or a pupil referral unit (PRU).

Long-term supply

I've been offered a supply job that will last one full term but I've been told that it can't count towards my induction. Why is this?

It sounds like the head teacher doesn't *want* it to count towards your induction rather than that it *can't* count. Head teachers do have to be in agreement before supply work can count, but it's reasonable for you to expect a full term placement to be inductable. It would be a good idea to request that the term is part of your induction period. You can do this in writing if it feels less confrontational. If this doesn't yield the result you want, contact the person responsible for NQTs at your LEA as he or she may be able to help. You could also ask your union for advice; the local or school rep may take up the case on your behalf and negotiate for you. If it turns out that the position is still not inductable, you may want to consider whether it's in your best interests to work there.

I'm working in a school on a part-time short-term contract and I am able to start my induction there. Can I fill in the days that I'm not working with short-term day-to-day supply?

Yes you can. If for example you are working three days in your part-time post, you can do short-term supply for the remainder of the week should you want to.

I've been at a school on short-term supply which has just been extended to the end of term. This means that I'll have been there for a full term. Does this mean that it can count towards my induction?

No. For supply work to count towards your induction it has to have been a full term in duration, whether part-time or full-time. You would also need to have agreed in advance with the head that the post is to count towards your induction and then all the necessary induction arrangements should have been kicked into place. You can't complete induction retrospectively or backdate it in any way.

> A full review of these arrangements is underway at the time of writing so it is worth seeing if very recent changes have been implemented yet by visiting the DfES website: www.dfes.gov.uk or TeacherNet: www.teachernet.gov.uk. You can also contact the DfES by telephone: 0870 000 2288.

I'm covering a teacher while she is on maternity leave for two terms. I have been told that I can complete two terms of induction but I feel insecure about the class. Do I have to stick to her rules and routines or can I do things my way?

This is always a difficult consideration for those taking over from a teacher for a significant period of time, but not permanently. It is fair to say that in the time you are teaching the class, they are your pupils and should do things your way. It's fine for you to create your own rules and routines with them and to introduce your style of teaching and learning into the classroom. You should feel free to arrange the room as you wish within reason and to create displays of the work you do with the children. However, it's also wise to find out as much as you can about the way in which their teacher taught the class and how things were structured and organised. You don't want your arrival in the room, along with any changes you may bring, to unsettle the class or classes to such an extent that you have a whole new set of issues to deal with in the form of disruption as they punish you for unsettling them by really testing out your boundaries! Aim to find out where the similarities are between the way you need to work and the way in which their teacher has worked with them and take it from there. As long as there is some common ground that the children will recognise, they will be able to cope with any changes you need to implement far more effectively.

If I'm completing a term of my induction while on a long-term supply placement, am I still entitled to a reduced timetable?

Yes you are. In effect you are a temporary member of staff and should have a 10 per cent reduction in the usual workload for teachers of your level in the school. This additional non-timetabled time should be used specifically for targeted induction activities. You are also entitled to a further 10 per cent reduction in your teaching load (that's 10 per cent of 90 per cent) and that additional non-timetabled time is to be used for planning, preparation and assessment (PPA). There is no flexibility for schools over their duty to provide NQTs with this non-contact time; it isn't optional!

There is extensive information about induction in Chapter 4. If you have any concerns about the way in which your induction is being handled, you should raise them as soon as possible with either your induction tutor, your head teacher, your LEA or your union. Don't sit on concerns without airing them.

Induction

I hear, and I forget. I see, and I remember. I do, and I understand.

(Chinese proverb)

Introduction

If you want to teach in a maintained school or non-maintained special school in England, you will need successfully to complete your induction period. This is often referred to as the 'NQT year' but for any working part-time or on supply it is likely to take longer than a year to complete.

Induction is crucial and shouldn't be underplayed. Unless you meet all the Induction Standards while continuing to meet the Standards for the Award of Qualified Teacher Status, you will not be able to continue your career in the state sector. It's that final. That said, the latest figures from the General Teaching Council for England (GTCE), which has responsibility for hearing induction appeals from those who are deemed to have failed their induction, show that up until May 2005, the GTCE had held forty-five induction appeal hearings and had five pending. Of these appeals, two were allowed, twenty-one were dismissed, four teachers had their induction extended by one term, twelve teachers had theirs extended by two terms and six teachers had theirs extended by three terms. Against the thousands of new teachers who successfully complete their induction each year, the number who fail, are unsuccessful at appeal and who have to leave teaching in maintained schools is very low. There is every chance that you will get through your induction with flying colours!

While this seems a tad tough on those who are newly qualified, especially considering that it wasn't that long ago when those fresh out of initial teacher training didn't have any such hoops to jump before launching their careers, it's worth remembering that induction has been designed to *support* new teachers and to ease them gently into the profession. It's far more about helping you to be the best teacher you can be than it is about stalling your career or trying to trip you up.

Induction is one of the main areas of concern for new teachers and I receive a vast number of enquiries about the induction period on a daily basis. The regulations may seem complicated but in reality, as long as you are aware of the most crucial points for you as a new teacher, you can let your school and induction tutor get on with the rest of it.

The following information applies to those who intend to complete their induction period in England. For those wanting to teach in the rest of the UK, the relevant education departments can offer assistance:

- Wales: www.learning.wales.gov.uk
- Northern Ireland: www.deni.gov.uk
- Scotland: www.scotland.gov.uk

FAQs in this chapter cover:

- Induction explained
- Starting induction
- Induction Standards
- Induction entitlements
- Extending the induction period
- Induction tutors
- The Appropriate Body
- Where induction can be completed

continued on facing page

- Induction in Wales
- Part-time induction
- Induction in more than one school
- Switching phases
- Induction abroad
- Induction in the independent sector
- Skills tests
- Induction and qualified teacher status
- Failing induction
- Induction and the GTC
- Completing induction
- Induction problems
- Taking a break from induction
- Induction and PPA time
- Induction tutor problems
- Induction observations
- Induction on supply
- Induction stress
- Formal assessments
- Unsatisfactory progress

All about the induction period

What is induction?

Induction is a period of time in which you will be working as a teacher, with all the attendant roles and responsibilities, while also demonstrating that you can achieve certain standards that have been set for new teachers. The period is basically a combination of specific and targeted support on one hand, and the opportunity for you to demonstrate your skills and continued professional development as a teacher on the other hand. It's about both monitoring *and* support.

Completion of an induction period is a statutory requirement for anyone who obtained qualified teacher status after 7 May 1999 and who wants to teach in a state maintained school or non-maintained special school.

Induction lasts for one full-time academic year (usually three terms) and this is calculated pro rata for those working part-time.

Do I have to start my induction period by a certain time?

No you don't. And once you have started your induction, you don't have to complete it in three consecutive terms. It's worth keeping in mind, though, that once you have started your induction period it is usually expected that you will have finished it within five years.

Where can I find a copy of the Induction Standards?

The Induction Standards form part of the DfES Guidance document on induction support. The latest version is, at the time of writing, ref: 0458/2003 and it can be downloaded from TeacherNet: www.teachernet.gov.uk. You can also find the Induction Standards in *The Newly Qualified Teacher's Handbook* (Routledge, www.nqthandbook.info).

What are my entitlements during induction?

- First and foremost, NQTs completing their induction must have a 10 per cent reduced timetable compared with other comparable teachers in the school. There is no flexibility on this – heads have a contractual duty to ensure that the time that new teachers spend teaching does not exceed 90 per cent of the timetable that other main scale teachers who do not have additional responsibilities teach. This time should be devoted to induction activities and not absorbed by planning or cover.

- NQTs are also entitled to a programme of monitoring and support. This must be tailored to your individual needs and should be designed to help you specifically to pass the induction period. This support and monitoring should be delivered around short-, medium- and long-term objectives which relate to your needs as a new teacher.

- You will be given a schedule of formal assessment meetings, usually towards the end of each term in a typical three-term year for a full-time NQT.
- Also during induction you are entitled to regular reviews of progress which will lead to termly reports on you. These reports, there are three of them, are typically prepared by the induction tutor in a school and sent to the 'Appropriate Body' (usually the LEA).
- An induction tutor should take you through your induction, making all the necessary arrangements for you and ensuring that all is well for you on a day-to-day basis.
- You should be given a named contact in your LEA with responsibilities for NQTs.
- You should also be given details on the nature of your contract of employment, a full list of duties and management arrangements and the school's health and safety and equal opportunities policies along with all the other relevant documents such as staff handbooks etc.
- As an NQT on induction you have certain entitlements to sick pay and contacts for further information about maternity leave, pension entitlements and salary payments.

Is it possible to extend the induction period?
Yes it is, under certain circumstances:

- If you have started your induction but haven't completed it within five years you can apply to the Appropriate Body for an extension (of up to one full school year).
- If you have been working through your induction period but have been absent from work for thirty school days or more, then induction would be extended by the aggregate total of absences. That means that if you have been off school for, say, forty days, your extension would be for forty days.
- If you have a break in your induction because of maternity leave, you can choose whether or not you would like to extend your

induction period by the length of time that you were absent on statutory maternity leave. It would be well worth contacting your union for advice on this at the relevant time if it applies to you.

What is an induction tutor?

An induction tutor is the person in a school with responsibilities for taking new teachers through their induction by coordinating, guiding and supporting your professional development. Once you have started your induction, your induction tutor will be the person who discusses with you how your non-contact time is to be used, who talks about your strengths and development needs with you and who makes any necessary arrangements that ensure that your induction is as successful as possible.

I've heard people mention the 'Appropriate Body'. What is it?

It's a strange title but it actually refers to the body that decides whether an NQT should be deemed to have passed or failed his or her induction. It is the Appropriate Body that has to inform the GTCE of the result of your induction and that can extend your induction. It also has to ensure that you are receiving sufficient support in the event of your experiencing difficulties meeting the Induction Standards. In short, the Appropriate Body has all sorts of duties, roles and responsibilities in making sure that you get through your induction and in supporting you if it looks like you might not make it.

The Appropriate Body for all maintained schools and non-maintained special schools is the relevant LEA. For independent schools, the Appropriate Body can either be an LEA (any in England) or the Independent Schools Council Teacher Induction Panel (ISCTIP). For sixth form colleges, the Appropriate Body can be any LEA in England.

Where can I complete my induction?

Not all schools can provide an induction programme for new teachers but the following types of school can:

- Maintained schools.
- Non-maintained special schools.
- Sixth form colleges (if an LEA agrees with the governors of the college that the LEA will act as the Appropriate Body).
- Independent schools under the following circumstances:

  - the curriculum for any primary pupils meets the requirements of the National Curriculum
  - the curriculum for key stage 3 and 4 pupils that you teach includes all core and foundation subjects
  - that there is an agreement between the school and an LEA or the ISCTIP that they will act as the school's Appropriate Body.

- Maintained nursery schools and independent nursery schools that meet the criteria for independent schools (the nursery has to have a head teacher and the induction tutor must have QTS).
- British schools in Guernsey, Jersey, Isle of Man, Gibraltar, and Service Children's Education (SCE) schools in Germany and Cyprus, which have induction arrangements identical to the English arrangements.

Can I complete my induction in Wales even though I trained in England?

Yes it is possible to complete your induction in Wales in schools which can offer induction under Welsh regulations for periods of a term or more. Any induction of a term or more which you complete successfully in Wales can count towards your induction in England and vice versa.

Can I complete my induction by working part-time?

Yes you can, although the length of time it takes is worked out pro rata. For example, if you teach half-time (0.5) then it will take two years to complete. Your head teacher and induction tutor should be able to tell you when you will be deemed to have completed your induction if you are working part-time.

Do I have to complete my induction all in the same school?

No you don't. Fortunately, for all those who complete their induction as supply teachers, it is possible to complete induction in more than one school. The only thing to remember is that induction can be undertaken only in jobs that last a full term or more. If you're just offered half a term's work, that won't be an inductable post.

If I have a part-time contract in more than one school, can I do induction in both schools?

Yes you can. It'll be complicated, but it is possible, as long as your contract with each of the schools lasts for at least a term or more. Just one head teacher and one Appropriate Body will take responsibility for your induction so you will need to make the necessary arrangements. Your union or the person within your LEA with responsibilities for NQTs will be able to help you sort this out should you run into any difficulties.

Can I complete my induction teaching in a primary school if I am trained to teach secondary?

Yes you can – in theory. QTS means that you are qualified to teach across the primary and secondary age groups and there is no legal requirement to retrain if you decide to switch age phases. However, the induction guidelines do state that NQTs should normally undertake their induction in posts that

- don't demand teaching outside the age range that they have been trained for

- involve teaching subjects that they have been trained for
- don't present acute or particularly demanding discipline problems
- involve teaching the same class(es) regularly, and using planning, teaching and assessment methods that other teachers in the school are involved in
- don't involve additional non-teaching responsibilities without adequate support and preparation.

I'm thinking of travelling and would like to teach in Australia. Can I complete my induction there?

No you can't. If you think that you'd like to teach abroad for a while, it is worth considering staying in the UK to get your induction period out of the way and then going travelling. That way you don't need to worry about induction on your return.

I am considering applying for a job in an independent school. Is it possible to do my induction there or will I just have to do it in a maintained school when I leave the independent sector?

It is possible to do your induction in an independent sector but only under certain circumstances. The school has to be able to fit the following criteria:

- the curriculum for any primary pupils at the school meets National Curriculum requirements
- the curriculum for any pupils at key stage 3 or 4 that you teach includes all core and foundation subjects
- an agreement has been reached between the school and either a LEA or, for schools affiliated to the Independent Schools Council Teacher Induction Panel, the ISCTIP that they will act as the school's Appropriate Body (this is the body that will oversee your induction). This must be arranged prior to the start of the induction period.

Before applying for a job in an independent school, find out first if they are able to offer an induction period for new teachers. Get this confirmation in writing if possible.

I've got GCSE maths and English. Do I still have to take the skills tests?

Yes you do. The skills tests are a requirement of the Standards for the Award of Qualified Teacher Status so without them you would not get QTS and would not be able to start your induction period. They shouldn't be a source of worry though; you can take them as many times as necessary. You can get further advice on preparing for and taking the skills tests from the Training and Development Agency for Schools website: www.tda.gov.uk.

Can I start induction before being awarded QTS?

No, it isn't possible to start your induction period before being awarded QTS. QTS is a requirement before being able to start induction and there is no flexibility on this.

I haven't yet passed all my skills tests but I have got a job to start my induction. Is this OK?

No. You need to pass the skills tests in order to satisfy the requirements for QTS and you can't start induction until QTS has been awarded. There's no way round this other than passing those tests!

If I fail my induction period do I lose qualified teacher status?

No you don't. Even if you fail induction you will still keep QTS as that relates to the Standards for the Award of Qualified Teacher Status rather than the Induction Standards. You would still be entitled to call yourself a qualified teacher but would not be able to teach in the state maintained sector (or in non-maintained special schools in England). In short, even if you fail induction, you retain QTS.

What does the General Teaching Council have to do with induction?

As an NQT you are required to register with the GTC while you are undertaking your induction. Then, when you complete it successfully, your Appropriate Body (usually the LEA) will inform the GTC, which then updates its teacher records on its Register of Teachers and issues an induction certificate.

If you fail your induction period, or are granted an extension by your employer, then the GTC will also record this on its Register of Teachers.

What happens at the end of induction?

Within ten working days of the end of your induction your head teacher must write to the Appropriate Body to give his or her verdict on whether or not you have satisfactorily completed your induction period. You should also receive a copy of this letter.

Then, within twenty working days of receiving your head's recommendation, the Appropriate Body must decide whether you have successfully completed your induction, whether you need an extension to your induction period or whether you have failed to complete it successfully.

Within three days of this decision being made and recorded by the Appropriate Body, it must write to you with the verdict (as well as your head teacher and the GTCE).

What happens if my head teacher and Appropriate Body decide that I haven't been successful in completing my induction? I'd just like to be prepared!

It's wise to be prepared! Although the chances of your failing your induction period are really very slim, it's important to know that you do have a right to appeal against any decision made about you.

There are very detailed appeal procedures that NQTs need to follow if they decide to make an appeal in the event of failing induction. These can be found in *The Newly Qualified Teacher's Handbook* and in Annex F of *The Induction Support Programme for Newly Qualified Teachers* (ref: DfES/0458/2003).

As well as becoming familiar with these procedures, it's important to remember to discuss your progress with your union, as it will be able to support you through the appeal process. Never feel as though you have to go through this process alone.

Problems

I've been told that I may fail my induction because I just don't seem to be able to get the discipline problems in my classes sorted out. I've found this year really hard and don't know how I'm ever going to pass. I feel sick every time I think about school and it's driving me mad thinking that all my studying so far may be wasted because I can't get through my induction. What can I do?

The moment your induction tutor and head teacher think that you may be at risk of failing, they should arrange for you to receive an increased level of targeted support. This means that if discipline is the big issue, you should be observed with your classes now, the specific problems should be identified and steps taken to provide you with help, advice and workable solutions that relate to you and the environment in which you're working. It's not only down to you to sort the discipline issues out: your induction tutor, head teacher and any other teachers who are acting as buddies or professional 'friends' should be stepping up the support that you receive. It would also be a good idea to talk to the person with responsibilities for NQTs at your LEA about it all. They should be able to oversee any additional support that you get to ensure that you have the best chance of getting through.

If you still have concerns about how your induction is being managed or about the risk of failure that has been discussed, you can talk to the induction team at the DfES about it. Contact them through the public enquiry line: 0870 000 2288.

I want to take a break from my induction but carry on teaching in the same school. Is this possible? I'd then plan to take up induction again after I've had a break from it all.

No, it's not possible to do this. Although you can take a break, you cannot teach in maintained schools or non-maintained special schools during that time if you are in a school where induction is available. You are 'obliged' to continue your induction while you can, or take a break from teaching in the above-mentioned schools. It's fine for you to do non-inductable short-term supply (see Chapter 3) during any break that you take as long as it doesn't take you over your four-term limit.

It might be worth spending some time thinking about why you would like to take a break. Are you managing your workload OK or could you do with some help in that area? Once you have started induction, if you are in an inductable post for the foreseeable future it's well worth ploughing on with it if at all possible. Take a break and you might lose momentum, so unless it's absolutely vital it's wise to carry on.

It's really common to feel overwhelmed at some stage of the induction year. There's a lot to get through and it can be emotionally as well as physically exhausting. If you feel as though you'd like to call a halt to it all, do talk to your induction tutor about how you are feeling. Aim to work out where you can release some time for yourself to restore some work–life balance and take a look at Chapter 9 – there will be some tips for you there!

I've been told that I can't have PPA time because I'm an NQT and I already get a reduced timetable. Is this true?

No! NQTs are entitled to a 10 per cent reduced timetable plus a further 10 per cent reduction in the remaining 90 per cent that they teach for PPA time. This means that they end up teaching a time-table that is 81 per cent of what a full teaching load for their level would be. This additional non-contact time cannot all be merged into PPA time: 10 per cent has to be used for induction purposes. Don't let anyone convince you otherwise!

Is it true that I will have to retrain if I don't complete my induction within two years of getting QTS?

No, that's not true. There isn't actually a time limit on when you must start induction by. And if you have started induction but not finished it, the usual expectation is that you will complete it within five years.

I really don't get on with my induction tutor. Is this going to be a problem for me? Is there anything I can do about it?

This isn't an ideal situation. The relationship that you have with your induction tutor needs to be as constructive as possible for you to get the maximum benefit from your induction. Your next move should ideally be a general discussion with your induction tutor about how things are going. Aim to work into this discussion a question about whether there is anything that you could be doing to improve your experience of induction. This will get the point across that your experience isn't the best it could be right now and that you're pre-pared to make any necessary changes. If this still doesn't lead the dis-cussion in the direction you need it to go, you can talk to the person within your LEA with responsibilities for NQTs to see if they have any local advice and knowledge that will ease things for you. If you feel comfortable approaching your head teacher you can do this too.

Be careful not to make any accusations; one way of avoiding this is to take the line of wanting to find out how *you* can improve the situation. I know that ultimately, your induction tutor should be able to create a working relationship with you that is as positive as possible, but sometimes, for a variety of reasons, this doesn't happen. It would also be a good idea to keep a written record of each problem or issue as it arises, and to seek the advice of your union. Don't let this slide. It needs to be addressed and sorted out sooner rather than later. You really don't want relationship issues to impact your induction period.

I haven't been observed at all so far since I started induction earlier this term. Do I just keep quiet about it or should I say something?

It's really important that you raise this with your induction tutor because, as an NQT, you do have certain responsibilities to make your concerns known in good time. It's a good idea to document your concerns for your own benefit and also any steps that you have taken to resolve them. During your first term of induction you should be observed fairly close to the start of the first half-term (and certainly within your first four weeks in post) and again in the second half-term. Thereafter you should also have two observations a term. Don't keep this quiet. This is something that needs to be addressed as soon as possible.

If you have any concerns at all about the way in which your induction is being carried out in your school, there are several courses of action you can take.

- You can talk to your induction tutor about your concerns.
- You can raise any worries you have with your head teacher.
- You can discuss things with the person with responsibilities for NQTs in your LEA.
- You can consult your union.
- You can ask for advice at Ask Elizabeth on www.eteach.com.

Whatever route you decide to take, be sure to keep a written record of your concerns, when you first had them and what you have done for yourself to try to resolve them.

I've had loads of observations but they never have a specific focus and I never get any follow-up. It's really frustrating. Is this normal?

No, that's not how observations should work. The whole point of being observed is to further your professional development. Each observation should have a focus informed by what you need to achieve in order to pass your induction successfully and your objectives for your development as a teacher. This is really essential – there's no point in 'blind' observations, they simply waste time and create negative stress. After each observation, you should have a follow-up discussion with your induction tutor. The purpose of this is so that you can both analyse what happened and the lessons that can be learned from it. A brief written record should then be made of the discussion you had which, the guidance suggests, should show any revisions that you decide to make in your objectives.

I've been told that because I'm doing a term of induction on supply that I can't be treated the same way as other NQTs in the school. This doesn't seem fair, is there anything I can do about it?

This isn't the case at all. Even if you are completing a term of induction on supply, you are entitled to be treated the same as any other permanent NQTs in your school. It would be worth talking this over with your induction tutor and if you still get the same message, take it up with the person in your LEA with responsibilities for NQTs. You may also like to discuss the situation with your union to see what advice you get. Whatever you do, don't let the situation slide. As an NQT, you have a responsibility to raise any concerns that you have in good time.

> See Chapter 3 for more information about induction and supply teaching.

I'm really stressed out about my induction period and whether I'll pass it or not. I'm dreading starting it as so much seems to rest on it. I just know I'm going to fail!

You really need to work at being positive about this! OK, some people do fail their induction but the percentages are incredibly low. The latest statistics on failures are shown in the table.

Table 4.1

Year	No. of induction results	No. of fails	% of fails
September 00 to August 01	20,521	30	0.15
September 01 to August 02	21,215	28	0.13
September 02 to August 03	23,071	26	0.11
September 03 to August 04	21,856	27	0.12

Looking at these statistics, you have a far higher chance of passing your induction than you do of failing it! Don't let it loom larger than it needs to. Get stuck into it and do your best, use the support that's available to you and aim to enjoy it. You'll learn a huge amount and are bound to develop as a teacher. The induction period is your time to consolidate what you have learned so far and to launch yourself into a career based on the notion of continuing personal and professional development. That's a really dynamic thought and definitely one to be positive about!

I haven't had any formal assessment meetings yet and I've nearly finished my first term. Shouldn't I have had one by now?

You should have three formal assessment meetings throughout the whole of your induction. For an NQT working full-time in a school running a three-term year (the most common at the moment) this means having a formal assessment meeting towards the end of each term. Check with your induction tutor that you have a meeting booked up for this purpose. The meeting can be either with your head teacher or with your induction tutor on your head teacher's behalf.

Although I've been observed a lot, I haven't had a chance to observe other teachers. Does this matter?

Your induction period should offer you the chance to observe experienced teachers. This can be either in your school or in other local schools. Observing other teachers is a really effective way of understanding more about the whole process of teaching, so if you don't have the chance to do it you'd be missing out on a lot.

Talk to your induction tutor about how and when this can be arranged. When you do observe other teachers, make sure that you have a focus for the observation that is linked into your development needs. For example, if dealing with low-level disruption is something you need to work on, make this your specific focus when observing other teachers.

I've been told that I'm making unsatisfactory progress. Does this mean that I'll fail my induction?

No, not at all! If you have been told that you're making unsatisfactory progress, you should also have been told exactly what your particular issues are and how you can address them to ensure that your progress improves and that you can pass your induction period. These points will help you if you have been told that you are making unsatisfactory progress:

- As soon as you are told this, the level of support that you receive should be stepped up with immediate effect. It is important to keep a written record of the additional support that you receive and when you receive it just in case you need to appeal to the GTCE at a later date. Any such written records will be invaluable.

- You must raise any concerns you have about the accuracy of the assessments made of you as soon as possible. You can do this by contacting the person within your LEA with responsibilities for NQTs. Again, keep a written record of any such communication.

- You should confirm with your induction tutor and head teacher the precise areas of concern in your work as a teacher. It should be possible to identify exactly what needs to improve and how this can be achieved. If it isn't, raise this with your LEA.

- You should have new and appropriate objectives set that will help you to achieve the Induction Standards.

- You should have had the consequences of not making satisfactory progress explained to you by your head teacher.

- If you have any additional concerns about the level of progress you are making and the support that you are receiving, you should discuss this with your union.

- If you think that the situation is causing you negative stress, discuss your symptoms with your chosen health care provider. You may also like to seek advice from Teacher Support Line: 08000 562 561.

- You can also get advice about your situation from the DfES induction team, which you can contact via 0870 000 2288.

CHAPTER 5

All about workload

Without deviation, progress is not possible.

(Frank Zappa)

Introduction

If there's one complaint you'll hear new teachers making, it's linked to workload. Despite the fact that NQTs get allocated time to devote to targeted induction support as well as additional non-contact time for planning, preparation and assessment, it can still *feel* as though there is an immense amount to do and very little time in which to do it.

In many ways it is just a matter of settling into the profession and finding out how you work, what your optimum pace is, how you can collaborate with colleagues in order to save time and how you can develop more effective and efficient methods of getting through your tasks in order for these feelings to subside. It's quite natural to feel overwhelmed at times – and teaching certainly isn't the only profession in which this can happen – but, like anything in life, taking one step at a time in the right direction can greatly ease any anxiety. You never have to tackle *everything* all at once.

Much has been written about teachers' workloads in recent years and a substantial amount of progress has been made in negotiations designed to improve teachers' conditions of service and their burden of work generally. New ways of functioning are developing in schools and it is likely that these innovations will continue over the coming years.

The questions in this chapter focus on the ways in which new teachers can manage their workloads more efficiently in order to create and maintain a supportive work–life balance.

FAQs in this chapter cover:

- Pacing yourself
- Prioritising
- Planning
- Time management
- Managing demanding times
- Using time twice
- Taking time off
- Procrastination

Am I the only one who feels totally exhausted by the end of each week? A weekend of two days just isn't enough for me!

I can promise you that you're not the only one to feel exhausted by the weekend! Many teachers experience the same thing and sometimes, it doesn't matter how much you try to pace yourself, the weekend just doesn't seem long enough.

It would be a good idea to look into time management to see if you can be more efficient in your use of time. *Teacher Well-being: Looking after yourself and your career in the classroom* (RoutledgeFalmer 2005) has plenty of ideas on this. Many particularly effective people talk of 'using time twice', meaning that they get the maximum use out of each minute that they get. It's also important to get to know how you work best. For some, a 'steady plod' gets them through the week whereas for others, blasting through their work in high energy bursts followed by clear breaks gets them through. What's best for you? Aim to have at least one weekday evening off and one full day every weekend where you do absolutely no school work.

Ideally you should aim for having two full weekend days off but, from the anecdotal evidence I receive from new teachers, this is often unrealistic during term time.

As well as determining what your natural working rhythms are, aim to identify when the real sink points of each term are. Every teacher experiences them and it's a good idea to avoid overburdening yourself at these times. Lighten up on the homework you set (to reduce the amount of marking you have to do) and aim to do activities that require you to keep things 'ticking over' as opposed to heavy planning and preparation night after night. It would also be wise to talk to your induction tutor about their perception of the pace that you are working to. Can they offer any shortcuts that you may be able to take? Are you reinventing the wheel unnecessarily? Watch how experienced teachers operate. What can you learn from them?

> You can find out more about pacing yourself in Teacher Well-being: Looking after yourself and your career in the classroom: www. teacherwellbeing.info.

Every time I try to pace myself something happens which throws me back into time poverty again. How can I avoid that? I don't seem to have any control.

I know that a lot is written about the need to control working life so that it doesn't control you, but the fact remains that it's impossible to control it totally. This leads me to believe that it's probably far healthier to develop the capacity to cope with the uncertainty that working life can create. If we're able to be resilient and flexible when it comes to the demands made of us we're more likely to be able to thrive at work.

Acknowledge that if you're flexible you're less likely to be thrown by unexpected events and demands on your time. Be aware that if something necessarily hijacks your time, and you agree to it having priority, you will need to adjust your expectations of yourself regarding other tasks on your 'to do' list. While we can't always exert *control*, we can be reasonable with ourselves about what we expect to achieve in a given time period. It sounds like a cliché, but to a certain extent we do need to develop the ability to *flow*.

How do I know if I'm working at my optimum pace?

The first thing to consider regarding pacing of work is that things *change*. Energy levels fluctuate over time, as does enthusiasm, and these two factors in particular can have a significant impact on what you can get done and at what pace.

That said, if you still think that you might not be working at your optimum, or most effective, level, you may like to go through these questions. Answering 'yes' to some or all of them could mean that you should spend some time exploring your management of time:

- Do I avoid beginning tasks because it all seems like too much?
- Do I allow myself time to plan what needs to be done?
- Do I spend time on tasks that are not essential?
- Do I allow myself to be interrupted by colleagues and pupils?
- Do I help others to achieve tasks at the expense of my own work?
- Do I view deadlines as constructive encouragement or a source of unparalleled stress?
- Do I struggle with tasks that could or should be done by someone else?
- Do I underestimate how long something will take me?

There are many approaches to time management to enable you to feel more confident about handling your workload. It's worth spending some time in your local library, bookshop or online exploring what's out there.

I seem to be hopeless at prioritising. Everything seems important! What can I do?

It might all *seem* important, but it shouldn't all have the same priority, otherwise you'll end up swamped under the pressure of it all and that's never the intention!

The easiest way of prioritising tasks is to make a *realistic* decision about whether they are of high importance, moderate, or low importance. Go through a prioritising process as soon as you can with each task so that you don't get that feeling of intimidation from them. Then stick to the priorities you decide where possible and work through them systematically.

Be aware of the 'trickle down' theory of time, that we place work at the top of our list, followed by our primary relationship, chores, social life and then, at the bottom of the heap, ourselves. Invariably this system doesn't work effectively enough for our health and well-being so we do need to devise personally satisfactory ways of *devoting* time to each of the areas of our life without relying on there somehow always being enough left over. There are no easy answers to this; if there were, we wouldn't be facing time management and prioritising issues. But we can work towards finding our *own* answers to suit our personal way of working and a simple awareness of our concerns about time and workload is a very good place to start.

> Remember that you can work any concerns about time and workload and development needs that you have into your induction plan and Career Entry and Development Profile.

Despite having successfully completed my training, I still find planning difficult to handle. Any top tips?

The best tip for handling planning is to find out exactly what the protocols for it are in your school. Use the wisdom and expertise of colleagues to make your task easier. There's no point in reinventing the wheel!

These additional points may also help:

- As well as the schemes of work pre-existing in your school, take a look at the schemes available on websites such as the government's Standards website: www.standards.dfes.gov.uk/schemes/. Schemes can help greatly with medium- and long-term planning.
- Aim to keep a balance between the amount of time you spend planning a lesson and the amount of time you spend teaching. Be mindful of what you can save or adapt for future lessons or classes. There's nothing wrong with reusing resources!
- Aim to do your short-term planning in blocks.
- Remember to keep records of what you have done with classes. Your short-term planning can be excellent for this.

> Planning is a skill that will develop over the course of your teaching career. It may seem time-consuming and all-encompassing now, but even after a term or two you'll notice how much easier it's getting.

I have a group of students in one class who seem to get through anything and everything I set for them. It's turning my planning into a nightmare but I'm really aware that I don't want to let these children down. What can I do?

Differentiation can be difficult to manage at the best of times and when you have quite an extreme of attainment to handle in one class, planning can become a challenge.

First of all, talk to your induction tutor about the amount and quality of work that you are setting. He or she may be able to suggest some new ways of extending and enriching it so as to keep these children satisfied for longer.

Second, think about doing open-ended projects around a theme (it's possible to do these with any age and any subject area) so that students take their work as far as they can take it. This is a great way of encouraging independent and responsible learning and can really show you just how much your class(es) can achieve. Again, your induction tutor, head of department or curriculum area leader will be able to tell you more about this.

You may also like to research what is available locally for gifted and talented children and young people. Does your school offer any additional study clubs or study support activities they can attend? Are there local summer schools for gifted and talented young people? Can they consolidate *their* learning by working with others in their class?

Whatever you do, be sure to harness this enthusiasm and take it forward to further their achievement and attainment, but do ask for advice and guidance so that you can utilise the expertise of others in your school rather than struggle on with the burden of planning for them alone.

The DfES Standards website has a whole area dedicated to gifted and talented young people where you will find heaps of ideas, discussion, best practice and guidance: www.standards.dfes.gov.uk/giftedandtalented/. You can also find out more at the website for the National Academy for Gifted and Talented Youth: www.nagty.ac.uk.

I've been told to work on my time management but I have no idea how! The simple fact is I don't have enough of it – end of story! What can I do?

This is a pretty universal problem for teachers to have! There's no doubt that teachers do, actually, have to achieve a lot in each hour of each day, but another factor in this is that the job has no obvious *end*. Teachers very rarely get to the point where every task is ticked off their 'to do' list and every aspect of their working life is perfectly in order. There is always *something* else to do!

The first thing to remember when it comes to time management is that you really need to know how you work. What's your style? Do you cover each term at a steady plod or are you happier with bursts of activity? If you don't know how you work most effectively, it's very difficult to devise strategies for managing your time. This is because your time management plan needs to be supportive of your working style and time needs rather than trying to fit you into a working style that just doesn't suit.

There are many time management solutions available from books to websites, interactive tools to courses. It's possible for everyone to learn more about time management and to improve their relationship with time. These general ideas may help for starters:

- Always be realistic about what you can achieve in any given time. Much easier said than done!
- You have a certain amount to achieve, but can it be split into short-, medium- or long-term goals?
- Does it help to write lists of tasks? Try assigning each one a time limit and stick to it.
- Keep your work spaces at home and at school as tidy and clutter-free as possible. Again, easier said than done for some of us!
- Remember that you can say 'No'! Or at least discuss your workload with your induction tutor. It may be that you can negotiate some time or resources to help you achieve a task.
- When you are working outside lesson times, aim to do it in a place where you won't be interrupted. It's better to devote a period of time solely to work, in order to free up time for quality socialising. Switch off your phone and limit other distractions.
- Are there any tasks you do that are really unnecessary?
- When planning what needs to be done in the long term, make sure that you build in some slack time, and certainly time for holidays and/or pure relaxation. Everyone needs time to catch up every now and then.
- Be sensitive to schedules in your school. If you're running out of time with anything, raise the issue as early as possible.
- Find out if your school uses electronic planners or schedules, or consider using any you may have on your own home computer or organiser.
- Collaborate as much as possible. There's no point in two people doing the same task when you can share the burden.

Above all else, get to know your warning signs of feeling over-burdened so that you can take steps to manage your time and prevent the onset of symptoms of negative stress.

> Optimus Professional Learning has a fully interactive professional development course for teachers on effective time management which you may find useful. Find out more here: www.optimusprolearning.co.uk. There are also many good time management books available on the market as well as websites to browse online. A good book to start with is Stephen R Covey's *First Things First* (Simon & Schuster 1994).

I'm interested in doing a time audit to see where my time goes. What's the best way of doing this?

There are several approaches that you can take (you can find out more in books such as Covey's mentioned above) but one simple way is to log what you do and when. Be totally honest with yourself and make sure that every minute of your waking day is accounted for. Then work out how much time is devoted to teaching, how much to other teaching-related activities, how much to socialising, to eating and food preparation, to hobbies, watching TV and so on. How are these activities spread through a typical day?

Then ask yourself these questions;

- Am I leaking time anywhere?
- Could I do certain tasks at different times of the day in order to be more productive?
- Could I regulate my time more effectively?
- What do I want to create time to do more of?
- Where can I get that time from?

Covey writes about the need to determine where tasks fit in his Time Management Matrix. This is a grid of four boxes: important and urgent, important and not urgent, not important and urgent, not important and not urgent. He gives examples of the kinds of tasks that can fall into each box. It can be useful to think about your management of time in this context too, so that you have another way of understanding where your time goes and how much you spend on the not urgent and not important box!

One important thing to remember about any time audit activities is that they are simply ways of gathering information about the way you are working. But that information isn't enough if it doesn't *inform* changes in your work practices in order to make you feel more time rich rather than time poor.

I can't believe I'm in this situation but just because I teach most of year 8 I've now got an impossible task ahead of me: reports! How can I get them all done in time? Most other teachers only have one or two year 8 groups and I've got seven! What can I do?

It would be reasonable to ask if you could have some additional non-contact time to spend on the reports. Do also ask other teachers if they have some time-saving tips for completing reports as they must be completed in your school. If the additional non-contact time cannot be arranged, ask for all the necessary paperwork to reach you as early as possible so that you can make a start immediately. Set yourself a goal of, say, five reports at any sitting, and work your way through them systematically. Leave any non-urgent tasks until after you have got through this monumental job and don't forget to give yourself a treat when it's all over!

I can remember reading about the idea of 'using time twice' but I don't know about how I might do that in my work as a teacher. Any ideas?

'Using time twice' is a way of getting more done in the time you have available by doing more than one task at a time. However, it's not for everyone! Some people find that aiming to focus on two things at once leads to increased stress and reduced effectiveness.

Just a simple awareness of what you're *actually* doing at any one time can show that we often use time twice without even realising it. For example, we may literally be sitting in a meeting talking about behaviour management but we're also listening to each other, expressing empathy and developing our working relationships.

It may be that you can implement the idea of using time twice in other areas of your life too. There are endless examples depending on what you like to do with your time for example, going running with a friend to catch up on news and work out together, asking your partner or a member of your family to help you out with some aspect of your school work to increase the time you spend together, or listening to a book on CD in your car to catch up on the reading you wanted to do . . . the list is endless.

I really feel as though I need a day off but I'd only be letting everyone down. What do teachers do when they feel like this?

If you're well, you should work. If you're unwell, and sufficiently affected to mean you need to stay in bed or visit your health care provider, you should have time off. If you feel as though you need a day to catch up, take a look at your management of time. Can you add in one task each day over the course of a week to see if you can catch up that way? It's amazing what effect this approach can have. Can you delegate some tasks? Can you ask for support or advice?

If you do need to have time off, don't feel guilty. It happens to everyone at some stage of their careers and that's OK! It would be far worse to struggle on ignoring all your warning signs, only to crash at a later date, requiring far more time for rest and recuperation. And your colleagues and certainly your pupils will really appreciate your staying away if you're full of cold and coughing your heart out! Just make sure that you follow closely your school's procedures for taking sick leave and if your absence becomes protracted, you may want to seek the advice of your union about making a return to work.

I find that I seem to procrastinate a lot whenever my workload feels too great. What can I do about that?

Procrastination affects us all to a greater or lesser extent and it can be quite paralysing. Then the more that turns up on our plate the less likely we are to tackle *any* of it, and so it goes on!

To a certain extent we have to be respectful of our natural ebbs and flows in energy and enthusiasm. However, while we should work *with* them, we can't be *ruled* by them, and sometimes have to override our 'slump' periods in order to get things done. These ideas may help:

- Don't put tasks off indefinitely. Either schedule them in for immediate or near future attention, or forget them if they don't need doing. Move on once you've made your decision.
- If a task is becoming a source of stress in your mind do *something* to start it sooner rather than later. As soon as you have taken the first step, it's far easier for the rest to follow.
- Learn to acknowledge the feelings of satisfaction that you get when a task is done and done well. Procrastination is the enemy of that feeling!

> Most guides to time management will also offer advice on beating procrastination.

CHAPTER 6

Behaviour

> The job of an educator is to teach students to see the vitality in themselves.
>
> (Joseph Campbell)

Introduction

Whether it is real or imagined, some areas of the media would certainly have us believe that the behaviour of pupils and students in our schools is heading towards anarchy! Despite the fact that Ofsted finds that behaviour in many schools is absolutely no cause for concern, there does seem to be a pervading belief that behaviour has taken a turn for the worse.

However, whatever the general trend may be, it is really irrelevant to you and your work in the classroom. This is because no two schools are the same when it comes to the way in which children behave, and no two teachers are the same when it comes to the ways in which they pre-empt, or respond to, the way their pupils are acting. The social dynamics between you and those you teach will be unique. That is why it is so important to acknowledge that behaviour management is as much about knowing *yourself* as it is about knowing your students. Your feelings and emotions on any day will impact the way in which your students respond to you and vice versa. Nothing happens in your classroom in isolation; it is possible to see connection in everything. Building an effective working relationship with your students is an ongoing thing – this isn't something that can be done by following some generic recipe and adopting a few quick tips when things go pear shaped. It takes devotion! That said, it's a way of life for an effective teacher, and openness to the ever-shifting relationships in your classroom can lead to an immense amount of job satisfaction, which, after all, is what it should all be about.

Something to consider when thinking about behaviour management is that the simple act of *acknowledging* with pupils what is going on for them can help to diffuse a good deal of tension. Evidence that you *notice* what goes on in school and in your classroom will go a long way. Another important factor in managing behaviour is never taking anything personally. The moment you do this you reach stasis in the situation and this effectively prevents forward movement.

This chapter looks at some of the more common issues raised by new teachers regarding the behaviour of those they teach. Don't be seduced into the trap of saying 'That wouldn't work for me'! If you are experiencing behaviour difficulties in your class(es) there will certainly be *something* you can do to improve matters and, while I can't promise that your answer will be here, what you read may help to trigger a solution that *will* work for you, in *your* specific circumstances. Be aware, though, that whatever techniques you adopt with your class, they should feel right for you and your personality. If there is a mismatch, your relationships won't flow with ease in the classroom and this could store up difficulties for the future.

FAQs in this chapter cover:

- Building working relationships with pupils
- Establishing ground rules
- School behaviour policies
- NQTs and 'difficult' students
- 'Nightmare' classes with reputations
- Behaviour and special educational needs (SEN)
- Circle time and behaviour
- Golden time

continued on next page

- Persistent low-level disruption
- Having to raise your voice
- Assertiveness
- Dealing with an angry outburst
- Group disenchantment
- Winning over a 'difficult' student
- Bouncing back after a bad day

What's the single most important thing I should remember about behaviour management when I start my new job?

Remember this and repeat it like a mantra . . . behaviour is all about relationships, and those relationships are subject to change. All kinds of factors can impact the way in which your pupils behave in your classroom. Some of these factors you can control or influence, and some you can't. There are no magic solutions, no list of top tips that will reduce your pupils to putty in your hands, but you wouldn't want that anyway! Perhaps the most important thing to remember is that there is no situation that cannot be improved upon. Everything changes, not least the way children behave and the way in which you respond to them. The way that you manage the behaviour of your pupils will develop over time. As a teacher, you are unique, and the best behaviour management tools and techniques will be those that you develop to suit your personality and teacher persona over time.

I'd like to spend some time getting to know my classes at the start of the school year but I'm also aware that I should launch straight into work, as there seems to be so much to get through.
Should I forget about introductions and niceties?

Absolutely not! The more time you can devote to getting to know your students and building solid working relationships with them the better. A relatively insignificant amount of time spent getting to know and like your students right at the start of the year can mean vast amounts of time saved later on in the term. Likewise, if you find that you are struggling with a class at any point in the school year, stop what you're doing and devote time to finding out why they aren't focused and what both you and the students can do to improve things. One or two lessons spent establishing and re-establishing your ground rules whenever necessary will help to ensure that both you and your students invest in the relationships in your classroom. The way in which you interact with each other is crucial to the quality of teaching and learning that can take place. Therefore, it's important to do all you can to keep the communication flowing between you. 'Introductions and niceties' are exactly what will help to enable you to work effectively as a team over the coming weeks, ultimately getting more work done.

My school has a policy of detaining students who misbehave but I don't think I really agree that it's the best thing to do. Can I devise my own methods for any students that need 'punishment'?

It's really important that you stick to the school's policy on behaviour management and don't strike off alone, doing your own thing. Students need to know that the policy is adhered to with consistency so even if you have theoretical or philosophical objections, you really have no choice but to go along with it.

However, it would be wise to use any time you may have with detained students to talk to them about their behaviour and discuss exactly why it is that they have been detained. Don't shy away from explaining why you need them to be cooperative and what impact it has on you, them and the rest of the class when they are not. You may not get anywhere first time, but persistent and reasonable discussion along these lines is known to have a positive impact on behaviour. This is particularly effective if you can see them on a one-to-one basis (although be cautious of being totally alone in this situation), as they won't be giving in to peer pressure to 'perform' in front of you. Use the detention as an opportunity to build a solid and secure working relationship with the student.

If you are still unhappy about detaining students, you could ask to talk about approaches to behaviour at the school with your induction tutor or head teacher (or any other teachers whose perspectives you'd appreciate). When the policy comes up for review, your thoughts may be taken into consideration.

Is it true that new teachers shouldn't be given students with behaviour difficulties?

It is true to say that new teachers shouldn't be given classes that present them 'on a day-to-day basis with acute or especially demanding discipline problems'. However, it is probably fair to say that at least some classes you encounter will contain at least one pupil whose behaviour you find a challenge, and yet this would be unknown until you start to teach them. The key is to pre-empt behaviour difficulties as far as possible, and to deal with them efficiently and effectively if or when they do arise. But don't feel that you must do this alone; utilise the skills and expertise of your induction tutor and other experienced teachers in your school, including any who may currently be teaching the child or who taught him or her in the past. It's impossible to guarantee that a class will be problem-free, especially when you consider the impact that the dynamics between teacher and class can have on the general atmosphere in the room, but it is possible to deal with any issues before they become too big.

I've been given a class that already has a reputation for being a bit of a nightmare. Sometimes I really struggle with them and often they just don't listen. I'd like to know just one thing I can do with them to make even a small difference!

Forget their reputation! Without a doubt, they'll be different with you. The trick is to make sure that they are better and not worse. Ideally, on the very first day that you meet the class, you should set up your rules and routines (and remember to express these in the positive, for example, 'listen to others' rather than 'don't talk'). If you haven't yet done this, it's never too late! Do this in such a way as to enable them to feel that they have chosen the rules – this kind of ownership can go a long way. Revisit them regularly and don't be afraid to reiterate exactly what standards you need in the room for you all to function effectively. Talk to your students about how you need things to be in the room and why. Ask them if there is anything you can do for them to enhance their enjoyment of school. It may sound as though this wouldn't have much impact, but this kind of consultation can work with children of all ages (and adults too) and should never be underestimated. It's certainly the best place to start. Most importantly, make sure all your students know what your signal is when you want them to listen to you. Do you say a certain phrase, stand in a particular place, clap your hands? Devise a signal and convey it to your class. That way there can be no doubt when you want their full attention.

If listening skills become a problem, there are plenty of activities that you can use to help remind your class(es) that the ability to listen is the basis of success in your classroom (and in life generally). Go over your listening rules (for example, one person to talk at a time, no interrupting and so on) and then devise activities within your area of the curriculum that will specifically sharpen these skills.

Spend some time working out what you think their learning styles are. We all learn in a number of different ways but some children in particular fall into one style more readily than others. For example, if you have pupils who find it hard to stay seated for any length of time, is there a way that you can work some physical movement into the lesson? Can you convey information visually? Or audibly? Do also tell the children that you have noticed that they find it hard not to get out of their seats and aim to work out a mutually agreeable way of helping them to work on that challenge. Work as a team and you're more likely to avoid the kind of confrontations that can be so stressful and draining.

Try not to carry with you the views that other teachers have formed on this group. Aim to anticipate problems before they manifest and deal with each one that does arise with fresh eyes.

Optimus Professional Learning has a fully interactive course on learning styles in the classroom as well as others on brain-based approaches to learning. These may help you to consider how you might adapt your teaching to suit the needs of those in your classroom with a view to improving behaviour. For further information visit www.optimusprolearning.co.uk.

I'm finding I have behaviour issues with some children who have additional learning needs. I think I just need to know more about how to deal with these needs rather than just responding to the behaviour of these children, but I just don't know where to go to for help. Any ideas?

As schools become more, rather then less, inclusive places, teachers are finding themselves dealing with pupils with increasingly diagnosed conditions. What would once render a child unsuitable for the mainstream is now pretty common in classrooms and this is generally thought to be a good thing. That said, if you have any children in your class(es) with additional learning needs it will be well worth spending a little time reading up on how you can best support them so that your lessons flow as well as possible.

Your school's special educational needs coordinator (SENCO) should be your first port of call. He or she should have the lowdown on each child's identified needs and suggestions on how to ensure that these are met in your classroom.

You may also like to read up for yourself if you have, for example, a child with autism or attention deficit hyperactivity disorder (ADHD) in any of the classes that you teach. There are some excellent books out there (a good quality high street bookshop or library will stock some of these) and, of course, the internet is worth a browse.

You're absolutely right to make the distinction between the *behaviour* and the *child*. The more you can do this, the easier it will be to ensure that effective learning takes place.

How can circle time help to improve behaviour?

Circle time has been around for a very long time as an educational tool but strictly speaking, it originated not as a way of solving problems, but rather as a way of developing more rounded individuals with effective interpersonal skills. Problem solving may occur as a positive by-product, but should not be the sole intention of creating circle time. It can also encourage an array of other positive outcomes such as enhanced self-esteem and self-worth, emotional literacy, self-regulation and control, tolerance and empathy, and a feeling of being part of a community that depends on cooperation for its success, among many others.

Those who advocate circle time in its purest form say that the teacher is not in control of the circle, but is there to *facilitate* what happens. For this reason, it is not appropriate to use circle time if you have your mind set on a particular outcome.

Circle time does not need to be long – for young children just fifteen minutes or so is sufficient, while older children will usually be comfortable with twice that or more. It's important that ground rules (or group norms) are set so that everyone knows exactly what is expected of them in the circle (most teachers use rules such as 'everyone is included as an equal', 'everyone gets to say their piece', 'talk about *issues* and not *people*', 'listen when another is speaking' and so on). For this reason, circle time can be an incredibly effective way of reinforcing effective learning at other times in your classroom and across the school.

Never underestimate how effective circle time can be with children and young people of *all* ages. This is not just a primary thing!

There are many books on circle time, and countless websites. But before settling down to a mega search session on the internet, ask around in your school to find out how, if at all, circle time is used. It will be most effective if there is some form of consistency across the school.

What is 'golden time'? How can I use it with my class?

Golden time is simply a way of rewarding good behaviour. It has been around for a long time but was probably less formally adopted in schools in the past than it is now. I can certainly remember being given the equivalent of golden time when I was at school!

In order for children to receive golden time (usually a fixed amount of time each week – for example, thirty minutes on a Friday afternoon) they must stick to the rules set (sometimes referred to as 'golden rules' and these may change each week depending on what the class needs to focus on at the time). Each time these are broken, minutes are deducted from the golden time. Usually this is done on a pupil-by-pupil basis so that the whole class isn't penalised for the behaviour of one or two individuals. OK, this may make it difficult to administer if you have to keep track of who gets what amount of time, but many teachers keep a running total on the board and find that it is well worth the effort of being fair in this way.

The most effective way of using golden time with your class is to make sure that they *want to do* the activities you are offering in their golden time and that it has a celebratory *feel* to it, and to speak to any pupils who lose golden time about this loss and what they think they could do to ensure they don't miss out in the future. This kind of 'follow through' helps to make it a learning experience.

Like circle time, golden time can be used equally effectively with primary and secondary pupils. OK, you may need to present it as a slightly more sophisticated concept with older students, but the concept is exactly the same – if you cooperate, you'll get a treat!

I feel that my classes are not as well behaved as they should be and yet they don't do anything majorly wrong. Why do they get me down so much?

You're not alone in feeling this by any means. Several research projects have found that it's not the major disturbances that get teachers down, it's the ongoing niggles and interruptions that become excessively tiring and remove any enjoyment from the job. It could be that you have very high expectations of how your classroom should run. While it wouldn't be appropriate to reduce your expectations, you may find that a slight adjustment will help to ease the pressure. Sometimes it's best not to fight every battle! That doesn't mean turning a blind eye; rather, it means assigning each situation the importance it deserves. At times, a quiet word at the end of a lesson to say that you noticed what went on and don't want to see that happening again can be far more effective than a public showdown that interrupts the lesson and spoils the peace in your room.

Revisit your agreed classroom rules and routines and if they don't seem to be adhered to, rework them with the group so that difficulties are raised and dealt with. This is like group housework – keeping things ticking over so that everyone in the room knows the boundaries and why they exist. It's not a once a year thing; healthy groups focus on the way in which they are operating on a regular basis. This needn't take hours out of your teaching time, but a few minutes devoted to raising and dealing with concerns about a group's, or individual's, behaviour is *always* time well spent. Be aware of when you need to talk to the *whole* group, and when just certain individuals need to be reminded of their responsibilities to themselves and to the group. Reinforce the kind of behaviour you want to see as much as possible and bring in those who are wavering, or simply not cooperating by asking them to problem solve or by giving them a specific task.

When you feel like this about a class it's easy to start dreading being with them, but aim to keep things light and bright before matters deteriorate. What *you* say goes, and isn't up for discussion, unless you set time aside specifically to focus on an issue in hand.

There are several good books on group dynamics and how group facilitators (or teachers) can ensure that they function more effectively. If you think that you would like to know more about this dimension of your teaching, it would be worth browsing a good high street or online bookshop for ideas, as well as your local library.

I'm fed up with shouting to make myself heard when my students misbehave, but what else can I do?

To a certain extent, the way in which teachers respond to behaviour can be partly a personality thing. Yelling at a class may suit some teachers but it certainly doesn't suit them all. It's also a clear indication that all is not well in that classroom and that emotions are running too high for comfort.

Aim to be aware of the full range of tools in your possession that you can utilise to regain control of a room. These include:

- *Your voice* – a calm, even delivery in a low rather than high pitch is most likely to bring the results you need.
- *Your body language* – even very young children can read body language and if your stance is defensive and closed, you're more likely to face that in your students. Avoid putting your hands on your hips or crossing your arms in front of your body.
- *Your facial expression* – sometimes we just don't need to speak words to convey our inner thoughts. Is your face giving away more secrets than it should? It's fine to express disapproval of a behaviour, but make your default expression a positive one, and never underestimate the power of direct eye contact as a means of asserting your authority.

I just don't feel assertive enough with some of my students. What can I do?

Assertiveness is an essential skill for teachers to have. It helps to convey your self-confidence and self-respect and yet shows that you are still open to the views of others. There are many ways of developing your skills of assertiveness from buying a self-help book on the subject to doing a course or joining a class. The following techniques can help when you feel the need to adopt assertive communication skills with your students:

- What you say and the way that you say it need to go hand in hand. Your body language and the words you choose should both demonstrate your assertiveness. Use direct language and address the issues surrounding the *situation* not the *individual*.
- Keep your body language open and friendly.
- Use simple language and don't be afraid to state what you want from the situation.
- Avoid being personal.
- Use 'I' statements – 'I would like to see you working, John'.
- Don't feel that you will be less popular by being assertive. If anything, the opposite will be true.

Optimus Professional Learning has a fully interactive online professional development course for teachers called 'Becoming More Assertive'. For further information visit www.optimusprolearning.co.uk.

Although it hasn't happened to me yet, I'm not sure how I'd deal with a child really flipping out in my class. What's the best thing to do when this happens?

Strong emotions can be very difficult to deal with in anyone, and perhaps more so in children and young people, regardless of their age. There are some easy steps to follow should this happen in your classroom:

- Safety of the child and his or her classmates, not to mention you, must come first. If you think the child may harm him/herself or another, send a child or classroom assistant for help as quickly as possible. Do not leave the room yourself.

- Don't get angry yourself – anger meeting anger creates a fiery mix. Stay calm and say calming things; simple statements such as 'everything's OK' can help to bring a situation under control. Keep your voice quiet and controlled.

- Keep offering a place outside the classroom for the child to go, even if this offer isn't accepted at first.

- Give the child the opportunity to 'get it all out of their system'. If this can happen away from the rest of the class, even better. Don't make demands; even if you sense imminent danger, issue clear instructions rather than hollering orders. Keep your body language, tone and volume calm and always give the space and opportunity for the child to respond to what you say (for example, if you ask them to sit down, make sure they physically have the room to do that without feeling you're invading their personal space). They may have lost it, but you can keep things light and controlled.

- *Always* follow up on strong emotional outbursts. While there may well be relatively simple reasons for the loss of control, the episode may be indicative of some more serious underlying mental health issues that should be explored sooner rather than later. Make a written record of exactly what happened, what led to it, what was said, what you did to try to calm the situation and what the outcome was. Discuss these notes with your line manager or head teacher.

It's rarely a teacher's fault when a child has an emotional outburst. More often than not the cause will be an accumulation of things that leads to a loss of control. Don't blame yourself, but if you feel shaken up by what happened, talk to a colleague or trusted friend.

I sometimes feel as though everyone in my class is playing up. It really gets me down. Any ideas?

This is a very common feeling, especially for new teachers, but it's important to realise that it's extremely rare for a *whole* class to play up. More often than not it is just a handful of key players, if that, while the rest of the group is probably as irritated by their behaviour as you are! This kind of reality check is essential, otherwise you can easily end up feeling that all your students are against you. Aim to identify exactly who it is during each session that is making life difficult for you as their teacher and for the other students. These are the ones to target, rather than the class as a whole, so make sure that you arrange time to talk to them either, as a subgroup or as individuals, about their behaviour, how it impacts the atmosphere in the room, and how they might work towards being more cooperative. While it's essential to be calm and reasonable when you have this kind of conversation, that does not mean that you need to be meek. Make sure that you know exactly what outcome you want from the conversation and state that to the child or group.

Recognise and acknowledge every single time they work well as a team. Tell them that you'd like to see that kind of cooperation more regularly so that they know exactly what kind of behaviour is acceptable. This isn't about being *authoritarian*, but it is about being *authoritative*.

There's one particular child in my group that I just can't get on with. Do I just bide my time until we don't need to get on with each other or try to improve matters?

It's *always* worth trying to improve your relationship with a child you seem to clash with. Don't blame yourself for this – we're all human and it would be unusual to get on with everyone equally well.

This checklist may help you to refocus on the positive strands in your relationship with this child and build on those for lasting improvements to the way in which you work together:

- Remember *always* to focus on the *behaviour* and not the *child*. Don't let it deteriorate into something personal. You'll have a far greater chance of success if you attempt to alter *behaviours* rather than *personalities*. It's easier to find something you *like* about the child this way too.

- Continue simple niceties such as greeting them by name with a smile.

- *Expect* cooperation and create opportunities for this child to succeed.

- Work at coming to a mutual understanding of what is wrong and how it might be fixed. Be aware that your view of the problem is likely to be different from their view. *Always* give the opportunity for the child to say his or her 'side'.

- Try to identify what *does* work with this child and find ways of replicating this as much as possible in your work together. Under what circumstances is this child most cooperative?

- What *really* interests the child? Can you use that interest in some way?

- Are there any aspects of this child's work or contribution to the school that you can positively reinforce?

- Take opportunities to speak to this child when you see him or her around the school. Just a quick chat about nothing in particular can help to break down barriers.

- Aim to find something that you have in common (for example, do you both love, say, bananas, football, rain or swimming?)

- Aim to find something that you like about this child and that you respect. Tell the child about this; positively reinforce this quality in him or her.

- Work on the child's self-*respect* rather than self-*esteem*. This can help to encourage resilience and resourcefulness and, in time, may help to bring round a previously uncooperative child.

- Make sure that the child can access the learning on offer in your classroom. Are there any simple adjustments that can be made to ensure that the child is able to concentrate more effectively (for example, can he or she read the board or hear OK, is the room too hot, too cold, too stuffy and so on)? Or is the child under-stimulated?

- Give clear instructions, broken down into basic stages if necessary.
- Create time to address any unmet emotional needs that could be impacting behaviour. Circle time can be a useful tool for this.

Remember not to spend so much time figuring out how this child ticks that you inadvertently neglect the rest of the class. It's always worth devoting time to creating better working relationships, but keep it all in balance.

You do not have to tackle major behaviour issues alone. There will always be someone experienced in your school who can offer insights and assistance so do utilise their knowledge if you need to. While it's important to remember that where behaviour is concerned, personalities play such a critical role, you will be able to pick up ideas from others and adapt them to suit your teaching style. Never struggle on alone; always ask for advice sooner rather than later.

I've had some really bad days with my class and sometimes I find it very hard to go to school in the mornings. Any ideas on how I can bounce back after a bad day?

You're halfway there by recognising that not all days are as bad as some are! When you feel that things just haven't gone as well as they could, for whatever reason, give yourself the space and time to take stock. What exactly went wrong? How might you do things differently in the future? Who can help you to resolve matters? Do you need to address any specific issues with your class(es) or with individual students? What will make you feel better about the events of the day? Can you identify the core of the feelings you are experiencing? Is it rejection? Or perhaps failure? Or disappointment? Or exhaustion? Even identifying this can help to remove some of its power over your emotions. Acknowledge the feeling, and what has led to it.

It's also worth thinking about whether there are other factors that have affected your resilience when you experience a bad day. Are you worried about anything? Do you have non-work pressures that are causing you to feel stressed? Simply identifying these can help you to understand just what you are up against and precisely where your stressors are. Be patient with yourself and talk things through with your induction tutor or another trusted colleague before letting events get on top of you.

Every teacher who has ever set foot in a classroom has had days that make them feel they'd rather not venture in ever again! But these are temporary feelings and just show that you're human, and responding to the difficulties and disappointments that working life throws up every now and then. Give yourself some time out for the evening, take care of yourself, have an early night and be prepared for feeling very different on a new day.

CHAPTER 7

Working with colleagues and parents

Laughter is the shortest distance between two people.

(Victor Borge)

Introduction

As an NQT not only will you be developing working relationships with the pupils you teach, but also you will be working closely with a range of other people including colleagues and governors, parents and other members of your pupils' extended families.

Usually, these relationships will be positively maintained without any problems but occasionally issues will arise that give cause for concern. Mostly these can be handled with a little diplomacy and a united front from the school.

This chapter explores some of the issues that new teachers have faced regarding the relationships they have with their colleagues and the parents and carers of the children they teach, and how best to deal with them.

FAQs in this chapter cover:

- Parental involvement in school work
- Communicating about behaviour
- Dealing with chatty parents
- Operating an 'open door' policy
- Critical parents
- Parent helpers
- Awkward situations
- Aggressive parents
- Complaints about homework
- Parent teacher associations (PTAs)
- Governors
- Assertiveness
- Workplace bullying
- Dominant colleagues
- Effective communication
- Working with teaching assistants (TAs)

Working with parents

I have a lot of very keen parents who want to be involved in their children's school work. How can I help them to feel involved without feeling that they are interfering?

There's a delicate balance to strike here. While it's fantastic to have such parental interest – some schools struggle to harness this – too much can be a little stifling.

Make sure that parents know when they can talk to you about their children and when they can come into the school. Encourage them to attend all the meetings and social events that your school runs and to get involved in the parent teacher association (see below). The aim here is to harness that interest and enthusiasm in a practical and positive way for the school.

You might also like to see if any parents have skills or talents that you could put to use in your classroom. For example, could any of them give a talk or run a workshop? It goes without saying that you should discuss any such plans with your head teacher first before going ahead and inviting a parent in, and that anyone who does work with children in your school, however briefly, should be checked by the Criminal Records Bureau.

Regarding over-zealous parental involvement in a child's school work, this is an issue usually best handled by a head teacher. If you have any such concerns, gather your evidence and present it to the head for him or her to take further.

I'd like to send some letters home to parents about behaviour (good and bad). What should I include in these letters?

It's important not to send any written communication home without first discussing it with your induction tutor or head teacher. Your school may well already have sample letter formats that you can either complete or use as a basis for your letters. In any communication with parents, think about what you want to achieve. What outcome do you want? If you're commenting on behaviour that needs attention, it's far better to request a time when you can discuss the issues face to face than commit complaints about behaviour to paper before they have been fully discussed with all concerned. Above all else though, it is essential to get the approval of your head teacher for any communication you send to parents. Don't think of this as a restriction of your professionalism as a teacher; rather, it provides you with an additional layer of support should any dispute arise as a result of your communication.

I'm a primary teacher and I find that there's a small group of mums that corner me after school just about every day. They seem to see it as a chat which I'd love to be able to do but I'm always thinking of the time it's taking and how much work I have to do before leaving for the day.

I don't want to appear distant and aloof but at the same time, I can't stand and talk about their children day after day when I should be preparing for meetings or doing my planning. How can I create a bit of distance?

It's hard to establish the balance between being available whenever there are problems or issues to discuss and keeping a professional distance between you and the families of the children you teach. Although your class may be on their way home, that is not the end of your working day and these parents need to respect that. One way around this is to establish a regular time when parents can drop in to the classroom at the end of the day to talk to you. They wouldn't need to make an appointment and you could say that for twenty minutes on every other Monday afternoon, for example, you will be in your classroom and available to discuss any concerns if necessary. If you find yourself being cornered in the playground, you can then remind them of your drop-in times and quickly extract yourself by saying that you're already late for a meeting. It's fine not to be available to everyone all the time. Clearly major concerns will need to be dealt with as and when, but by adopting a drop-in time, you'll be able to contain the chatterers a little more and create some balance and space for yourself.

One parent in particular is making my life a misery. She criticises me constantly and I feel totally undermined by her. What can I do?

Many teachers have had this experience at some point in their careers and it can be stressful and demoralising. Whatever you do, *don't* take it personally! It's important to alert your line manager and/or induction tutor about what's going on. Her comments should be listened to, but if you ever feel that they are unfair or unreasonable, calmly state that you will raise what she has said with your manager and a meeting will be arranged during which these matters can be discussed.

Comments from parents should be listened to but don't necessarily have to be taken on board if they have no grounding in reality. It could be that your head teacher could talk or write to her to come to some understanding.

Above all else, do not let incidents like this undermine your confidence in your abilities. If anything, use them to confirm to yourself that you know what you are doing and are justified in taking the actions you take. Criticism can be great if it's constructive – after all it helps to propel us towards making improvements and becoming more effective in whatever it is that we are doing – but constant undermining serves no positive purpose and you don't have to tolerate it.

> If you feel that this situation has not been handled sufficiently by your managers, and it has not been resolved satisfactorily, you may want to discuss matters with your union.

Some of the parents of children in my class have asked if they can help in the classroom. I'm not keen at this point in my career but feel I ought to say yes. Any ideas on dealing with this so I don't offend anyone?

The first thing to consider is, what is your school's policy on having parent helpers in classrooms? Some are very keen while others prefer not to encourage this. Don't do anything at all without first discussing it with your head teacher.

If you do decide to make use of this offer of help, and your head teacher is in agreement, talk to your induction tutor about it. Perhaps you can identify some tasks which could usefully be done by a parent while you get on with teaching. Remember that they would have to go through a Criminal Records Bureau check to make sure that they are suitable to be working in your classroom. It would also be a good idea to discuss closely with any parent helpers exactly what it is that you want them to do, and how to do it. You may like to keep a notebook with a list of tasks they could be getting on with that they could refer to each time they visit your classroom. It's also a good idea if you can arrange a regular time that they turn up, so that there is some structure to the help they are giving you. Remember, though: don't do anything with any offers of help without discussing them in detail with your head teacher. There are child protection issues which need to be considered.

However, if you really don't want to accept any offers of help, then you can politely decline them *for the time being*. That way you are not saying *never* but you are buying yourself time until you feel more confident about using additional help in this way.

I was recently in a situation where a parent behaved in what I would describe as an inappropriate way. I had no idea how to deal with it. What should I have done?

It is never acceptable for a parent to put a teacher in a position that they feel is inappropriate. You do not have to tolerate that, although I appreciate that it can be difficult to deal with at the time.

If that happens again, politely remove yourself from the situation (give an excuse, for example, being late for a meeting) and make a written record of exactly what happened, what was said, what was intimated and any actions that took place. As soon as possible, report the incident to your head teacher. You may also like to seek advice from your union.

You should expect total support from your head teacher in resolving this issue. It could be that the parent is communicated with about the incident, but whatever happens, you should feel safe and supported. If you don't, it will be advisable to discuss the matter with your union. Never feel that you have to just put up with this kind of behaviour. It should always be taken seriously.

The parent of one child in my class is known to be aggressive. I have to meet him about some issues that have arisen regarding his son. Are there any points I should remember when I do this? How should I handle it?

This probably won't happen much in your career but you're wise to be aware of the risks when it does. If this parent has a history of aggressive behaviour you should not be expected to meet him on your own, and it would be perfectly reasonable for you to request that another member of staff be present when you do meet.

As a teacher, you do not have to tolerate *any* level of aggression directed at you by a parent. It is *never* acceptable. These precautions can help you to avoid being in a situation where aggression may arise:

- Put your personal safety first. Always meet in a public area rather than behind a closed door and aim for you both to be seated.
- Always have a third party present.
- If the discussion deteriorates and you suspect that anger and aggression may follow, terminate the meeting and explain that it will be better for you to talk another time.
- Don't feel that you have to change or soften what you say for fear of a reaction from the parent. If you are reasonable and can back up everything you say with examples, you are perfectly justified in saying it regardless of whether the parent wants to hear it.
- Aim to work in partnership for the benefit of the child.
- If you think an encounter with a parent has been aggressive or violent, report the matter immediately to your head teacher and make a written record of exactly what happened. Ask your witness to do the same. The matter should be handled by the head teacher. You may also like to seek union advice.

It's always going to be best for the child if channels of free communication can be kept open between the school and a parent such as this, but you do not have to risk your personal safety in order to achieve this. Be aware and take precautions!

One parent has complained that I don't give their child enough homework and yet I carefully stick to the school policy on homework. Should I give more work to this child?

It's a good idea always to refer complaints such as this to your head teacher. As long as you have been following your school's policy on homework, which will have been conveyed to parents, you should receive your head teacher's full support.

I would advise against treating this particular child differently by setting extra homework. However, after discussing the matter with your head teacher, you may decide to set some extension work for this child to do. This should not be work that requires you to spend additional time on marking and assessment, but it could appease the parent and nurture the child's interest in his or her work. That said, any such arrangements should be fully discussed and agreed between you, the parent and the head teacher and should not add unduly to your workload. If you're abiding by your school's homework policy, this should be your call.

I've been asked if I want to join my school's PTA. What exactly is it?

A PTA is a parent teacher association. Most schools have them and they plan and run fund-raising events for the benefit of the school. Some PTAs are very active, supplying the school with additional resources and funds. A well-run PTA with committed members can make a tremendous difference to school life for both teachers and pupils. The latest figures available show that PTAs in England, Wales and Northern Ireland raised £73 million for schools in 2004. That's pretty impressive!

You're not obliged to join your school's PTA but membership does carry certain advantages, not least the opportunity it provides for getting to know some of the parents of the children that you teach and having a say in how funds raised are spent on the school. However, if you think that attendance at PTA meetings will be a burden too far, it might be an idea to decline the offer for the time being. You could always sit in on a meeting to see what is involved with a view to joining the PTA at a future date.

Working with colleagues

I don't actually know what governors do. Should I know or will I not ever have anything to do with them?

Every school in the maintained sector has a governing body. These bodies have far-reaching powers and responsibilities and it is important for all teachers to know what they do and who their governors are, as even if you don't come across governors in your day-to-day work, their decisions will undoubtedly impact the way that you work.

The Newly Qualified Teacher's Handbook identifies the following as just some of the roles that governing bodies have:

- The main role of governing bodies is to aid in the raising of standards in a school, including creating plans for the school's development. This entails ensuring that pupils at the school are offered the best education possible, through effective management and correct delivery of the National Curriculum and religious education, assessments and target setting.
- Governors must also ensure that the school has a character in line with its ethos and mission, particularly in voluntary aided schools. To do this, they must determine the aims of the school as well as the conduct, and appoint, promote, support and discipline staff (including head teachers and deputies) as appropriate. They also set the times of the school day, and the governors in foundation and voluntary schools can set term dates as well.
- Governors have a role in deciding how best the school can promote the spiritual, moral and cultural development of pupils.
- Governors must manage the school's budget in accordance with current education law.

> You can find out more about governing bodies from *The Newly Qualified Teacher's Handbook*: www.nqthandbook.info. You may also like to look at Governornet for further information: www.governornet.co.uk.

I've been told that there's a governor attached to my department who may want to come in to my classroom to observe some lessons. Why would a governor want to do that?

Governors have a role of being a 'critical friend' to a school and part of that will entail monitoring what goes on in the classroom. The best way to do that is to observe lessons, and many governing bodies will divide the curriculum areas up between them for this purpose. Some even like to get involved in a more hands-on kind of way.

Although technically a governor can drop into a lesson at any time, it would be usual for prior arrangements to be made. The last thing a good governing body would want is for teachers to feel that they are being 'picked on' or 'spied on'. The relationship between governors and teachers has to be one of mutual respect for it to work most effectively.

If a governor does come into your classroom to observe, it is perfectly reasonable for you to ask what the focus of the observation is and to offer access to any resources or worksheets etc. that may help inform the observation. Aim to treat the situation as being mutually beneficial. You should both be able to gain from it.

I find it really hard to be assertive, even when I know I should be. What can I do? I don't want people to walk all over me!

It can be understandably hard for new teachers to assert themselves when they have joined a school community and are not yet fully settled into the way things run. Yet even when it feels uncomfortable, it is better to be assertive than passive, if you end up resentful over not speaking up for yourself!

Teacher Well-being: Looking after yourself and your career in the classroom reports that people who communicate assertively will often

- initiate and end conversations when appropriate
- change the direction of a conversation if it is compromising their rights, feelings or opinions, while respecting the other person

- face up to and discuss issues and problems that are adversely affecting them
- question authority when appropriate
- openly express emotions and opinions
- say 'No' when too much is being asked of them
- use ordinary conversational tone in communication with others
- use respectful language to make a point
- match facial expression with the words spoken to avoid mixed messages
- use body language to indicate openness and friendliness
- engage and participate in group situations.

Can you take any ideas from that list?

I feel really intimidated by one particular colleague. Someone suggested that they might actually be bullying me. Is there anything I can do about it? It has really affected my confidence.

Bullying in the workplace does go on and it can be hard to recognise at first. If you think that you may be experiencing bullying at work these steps will help:

- Talk to a trusted friend or colleague about what is happening. Ask specifically for their opinion and perspective.
- Talk to your induction tutor about what is happening.
- Read your job description so that you know exactly what you are supposed to be doing at work.
- Read up about assertiveness (see page 106) or attend a course on assertiveness.
- Contact your union for advice on dealing with bullying at work.
- Keep a record of all communication you have with this colleague.
- Be sure to refute all unfair claims made against you.
- Monitor changes in your work performance that you think might be down to the treatment you are receiving from this person.

You do not have to put up with bullying and intimidating behaviour from colleagues. If you think that your health may be suffering, register your concerns with your chosen health care provider. Don't struggle on alone without seeking help. Workplace bullying is illegal on several grounds and, if you raise the issue with your induction tutor and head teacher, they should ensure that the situation is dealt with.

You can find out more about workplace bullying from www.bullyonline.org.

I am due to start my NQT year in September in a school nursery and although I'm really looking forward to it, I'm a bit worried about the nursery nurse who I'll be working with. When I met her she seemed very nice but she's studying for her degree so that she can do a PGCE and has a decade more experience than me. Her ideas are great but I felt that she was very dominant. I'd like to talk to her about it but don't know how to do it tactfully. I want her to realise what the boundaries are but I'm dreading making an enemy out of her.

There are several approaches you can take with this. You could do nothing and just wait and see how things turn out, or you could broach the subject in a fairly light-hearted way and say something like: 'It's a little daunting having someone so experienced to help me'. That way you are positioning yourself as the one in charge yet respecting the fact that she has such a lot of experience. This could really work in your favour. It will be great having someone like that to draw on. As you have already detected that she seems to be dominant, I would give her plenty of 'positive strokes'. People like that tend to need to have their achievements recognised and the more you can show that you respect her and what she's done, the less she'll want or need to remind you of it! Ultimately, if things don't work out, you can discuss it with your induction tutor, but if you can aim to develop mutual respect between you, that will be the best outcome.

I sometimes feel as though I don't actually get on very well with some of my colleagues. How can I communicate more effectively?

It can be difficult to maintain good relationships with colleagues when you feel busy during your working day and that every minute counts. *Teacher Well-being: Looking after yourself and your career in the classroom* suggests the following points to help to ensure that your communication with colleagues is as positive as possible:

- If you have a valid reason to 'moan', there will be appropriate routes through which to make this known so a solution can be sought. This might be through discussing the gripe with your line manager or mentor, or adding it anonymously to a suggestions box. Whatever you do, don't bash on about it incessantly in the staffroom! It may sound obvious, but even when others agree with our moans, they won't necessarily want to hear about them.

- Observe how you feel about certain styles of communication. Watch how others interact and notice if you behave differently when in the company of particular colleagues. This all helps to determine how best to communicate with others for the best possible outcome.

- Be true to yourself in your interactions. Coming from a point of stability and honesty is important, even when you don't perceive all others doing so.

- Keep an eye on the style of language you use in your communications with others. Subtle changes in the words we use can have an impact on the way in which our message is received. For example, do you ever exaggerate to make a point? Do you focus on the problems and not on the potential solutions? Is there a willingness for flexibility in your language? Do you use limiting words?

- Show others that you are able to see the pros and the cons of a situation.
- Don't let conflict situations slide without making the effort to resolve them sooner rather than later.

You can read more about communication with colleagues in *Teacher Well-being: Looking after yourself and your career in the classroom*, www.teacherwellbeing.info.

I'm fortunate in that I have a teaching assistant with me most of the time but I don't know how to make the most of this situation. What should I be doing?

Having an additional adult in your classroom can be brilliant and a great way of ensuring that your pupils really get the most out of their time when you teach them.

Your school may well have a policy on how teachers should work with their TAs (and vice versa) and if it does, this should be your main source of inspiration. If it doesn't, these ideas may help:

- Make sure that you are clear *why* the TA is working with you.
- Be sure to share your classroom rules and routines with your TA so that he or she can reinforce them too. It's important to present a united front.
- Discuss your mutual expectations with your TA.
- Consider preparing an information sheet for your TA.
- Be very clear about your intentions.
- Use a notebook to communicate with your TA for the times when you don't actually get a chance to talk.
- Meet regularly, even if only for a few minutes, to discuss how things are going and whether any changes need to be made in your working relationship.
- Be aware of how your TA can observe your progress through your induction period. His or her feedback could be really useful to you.

The teaching assistant section of Teachernet is packed with useful information. You can find it here: www.teachernet.gov.uk/teachingassistants. The publication, *Working with Teaching Assistants: A good practice guide* can be ordered free of charge from the DfES publications order line: 0845 60 222 60, quoting reference 0148/2000.

CHAPTER 8

Getting through the year

We are what we think. All that we are arises with our thoughts. With our thoughts, we make the world.

(Buddha)

Introduction

With so much focus on reaching and maintaining certain standards, planning and preparation for all your classes, managing behaviour, attending meetings, observing and being observed, and generally settling yourself into your new career, the crucial matter of maintaining a work–life balance can plummet right to the bottom of your list of priorities.

While it's natural to want to focus so much on work – after all, it can seem as though you have no choice given all you have to get through as a new teacher – the need to keep at least half an eye on the quality of your life outside school cannot be overemphasised. Yes, you're a teacher, but that is just one dimension of your life among many others. It's important to give your induction period all you can, and to commit yourself to the career that you have chosen, but *you* the *person* need attention too.

I get a huge amount of emails from new teachers who are struggling with their work–life balance. It certainly seems to be one of the most challenging dimensions of early life in the teaching profession, setting up potential danger points at which it can seem easier to just walk away than to continue the struggle. And yet, despite the fact that the job is still highly demanding, both physically and emotionally, progress has been made in recent years in addressing the work–life balance of teachers.

If you get one thing from the chapter that follows, it should be that you never have to struggle on alone when you are experiencing overload at work. There *are* sources of help for you and there is no problem that cannot be explored, handled and overcome in some way. Don't, whatever you do, reach a point where you feel defeated before seeking some of the help and advice that is available out there. You don't have to choose between work *or* life. You can have both, even if at times you may be juggling and struggling. And to strive for both is important if you're to be an effective teacher. All work and no play and all that . . .

This chapter covers the issues that typically come up around work–life balance and some of the effective solutions that you might like to employ if this is an issue for you.

FAQs in this chapter cover:

- Avoiding getting run down
- Boosting your immune system
- Working all hours
- Getting ill at the weekend
- Voice protection
- Recognising negative stress
- Panic attacks
- Work–life balance
- Irritable bowel syndrome (IBS)
- Feeling tired all the time
- Perfectionism

Maintaining well-being

I'm in my second term of induction and really want to avoid getting run down. Towards the end of last term I felt so tired. How can I avoid that?
This is so common among new teachers but needn't be the inevitable outcome of every term that you're a teacher. It's all about pacing. This can be very hard to achieve when you're working through your first term of induction as so much is unknown, but there are still things that you can do to make sure that you don't start to burn out at the end of every term.

School days, terms and years have very distinct rhythms. Becoming familiar with these and aiming to work with them rather than against them will help you to preserve enough energy to take you right through to the end of each term rather than running out of steam and risking burnout as the final weeks of a term approach. These points may help you:

- Make sure that any goals and targets that you have for each day are *achievable*. It's not about doing all that you think needs doing. It's about prioritising and having realistic expectations of yourself.
- Take any help that is offered to you. There's no point in reinventing a wheel, or lesson plan, that works perfectly well.
- Aim to identify time and space that you can reclaim as your own. Identify where your biggest commitments are through a term (exams, reports, assessments, observations and so on) and aim to ease your workload at these times by not taking on anything that isn't essential.
- Be aware of how each week pans out for you. Which are your nightmarish days? Can you ease these in any way by leaning on pre-prepared work, help from learning support assistants (LSAs), and so on? What day is your lightest one? Is there anything that you can save from heavier days to do on your lightest day?
- Do you know when and how you work most efficiently? If that's between, say, 6pm and 8pm, don't struggle with preparation and

marking at 4pm when you might naturally need to take a break and recharge. Learn to go when you have the energy and stop when you don't. Everything will get done.

- Plan in relaxation treats (whatever does it for you) at regular points through each term. Delayed gratification isn't going to work when the demands you're making of yourself are high. Regular rewards are more likely to keep you going.
- Finally, if you need a break, take one. There are no prizes in this world for working so hard that you crash and burn.

> Pacing yourself has a lot to do with time management too. You may also want to look at the information on this in Chapter 5.

I seem to catch every bug going. As soon as I'm over one cold I catch another one! Whatever the children seem to have I come down with and it's making me feel as though I'm not up for the job.

This is not at all unusual when you start out in the teaching profession. Not only will your immune system be affected by the additional stresses you'll be feeling linked to starting a new job and needing to be successful in your induction, but also it is facing an onslaught of alien bugs and germs from a whole load of new people you're not used to mixing with. That's quite a lot to be dealing with!

It's important to be aware that any symptoms that you experience are evidence that your body is fighting to rebalance itself. Your body is conveying a message to you and you owe it to yourself to listen.

It would be a good idea to take some steps to boost your immune system so that you can be as armed as possible in the battle with those bugs. These ideas can help:

- Increase your intake of antioxidants as these help to boost your immunity. Vitamin A strengthens cells that keep viruses at bay and Vitamin C helps to fight them when they get through.

Zinc and selenium are important too. You can buy good quality antioxidant supplements from specialist health food stockists. If you'd rather do this through diet, simply increase your intake of apples, oranges, red, green and yellow vegetables, carrots, potatoes, grains, seeds, nuts and cereals.

- Take an immunity boosting supplement such as echinacea, aloe vera, garlic or bee pollen. Seek expert advice on this (from a specialist stockist or practitioner) if you have not tried this approach before.
- Keep your lungs as healthy as possible by exercising or even singing!
- Give yourself time to exercise each week. Do something that you enjoy, then you're more likely to continue to do it.
- Drink plenty of water all through each day.
- Get rest when you need it.

Don't ever feel that you're somehow weak because you're sometimes susceptible to bugs. Your immune system is bound to strengthen over time and if you talk to any experienced teacher, they'll almost certainly say that they too caught every bug going when they started out. You're not weak, just human. But there's plenty that you can do to support yourself.

Any persistent symptoms should be checked out by your chosen health care provider. Don't struggle on with symptoms indefinitely as they may have an underlying cause. For example, fatigue can be a symptom of diabetes, ME and depression among many others. Get yourself checked out sooner rather than later.

I find it very difficult to know when to stop working for school. I live alone and so I can easily spend the whole evening on school work and it really gets me down sometimes. How can I get some life back?

It's not uncommon for teachers who live on their own particularly to do excessive amounts of work in their own time. There are few if any demands on their time when they are at home and it can be easy to carry on working if real efforts aren't made to ring-fence down time.

Ideally, you need to be able to take an evening off at short notice when the need arises. This means you need to be as well prepared as possible in terms of your forward planning so that you can give yourself some slack when you need it. The following ideas may also help:

- Work at maintaining good relationships outside work. If you make arrangements with friends, stick to them, don't cancel at the last minute. Sometimes having something else to do in your spare time can really mean that you focus well in your work time.
- Aim to keep spontaneity alive and well in your life! Allocate time for what you know you want, or have, to do, and leave a little spare for who knows what?!
- Make sure that at least 75 per cent of your holidays are work free.
- Work out how much time you are not required to be in school. This is the time that you have control over. The first rule of well-being is to recognise where your control lies.
- Aim to pursue a hobby, even if this is simply keeping fit.

I always seem to feel ill on a Saturday. Just when I really need my time off I seem to spend it either with a cold or a headache. What can I do?

What you're describing is what's known as 'leisure sickness'. It apparently affects quite a chunk of the population, and in particular those with a heavy workload, perfectionist tendencies and a strong sense of responsibility. It seems that certain types of people put off being ill until they have time for it!

There's really only one way of avoiding getting ill at the weekend or when a holiday starts and that is to take care of your health and well-being on an ongoing basis. You need to listen to the symptoms your body throws out as soon as you notice them. Don't deny them; if you do, they'll stay in check until your next day off! Take sick leave when you need it and be careful to plan in relaxation time as often as you can.

I was told that I have to develop some strategies for commanding silence in my classroom as I have a quiet voice. My tutor suggested a whistle, but my classroom is open-plan and that doesn't feel right to me. What can I do?

It is possible to strengthen the voice, but you might want to consider asking your GP if you can be referred to a speech therapist for specific advice for your needs.

Ideas that are known to have worked for teachers include:

- putting one hand right up in the air to indicate when you want silence
- clapping your hands very loudly just twice (you could do this just before you raise your hand in the air so that you are giving a visual as well as an auditory signal – particularly useful for those who may not be facing you when you want their attention)
- using a tambourine
- having 'quiet days' when everyone in the room uses the lowest volume to communicate to raise awareness of noise levels in the room
- using a small bell or (as has been known) a bicycle horn!

There is a good deal of advice about voice strengthening on the Voice Care Network website: www.voicecare.org.uk, as well as in *The Newly Qualified Teacher's Handbook*: www.nqthandbook.info and in *Teacher Well-being: Looking after yourself and your career in the classroom*: www.teacherwellbeing.info.

Stress busting

My boyfriend thinks I'm stressed out all the time. I don't think I am but he thinks I'm just not recognising it. How would I know if I was stressed?
It can be easy to spot when someone else is stressed out but far harder to recognise the symptoms of stress overload in ourselves. This is because when in the midst of chronic stress, we rarely lift our heads high enough to notice what's actually going on for us; we're simply too busy!

Stress, or to be more accurate, *negative* stress, can manifest in many ways, but there are some classic signs and symptoms to watch out for. The signs of excess stress can be physical or mental/emotional and while they may not all appear in the same person at the same time, it's important to be alert to the following possibilities:

In the body:

- the blood supply to the muscles increases
- the adrenal glands produce more adrenaline
- pupils become dilated
- the heart rate increases
- blood pressure can rise
- the sweat glands can produce more sweat
- breathing becomes rapid or troubled, with hyperventilation
- swallowing can become difficult
- muscles can become tense and rigid
- blood-sugar levels can rise

- frequency of urination increases
- frequency of headaches and migraine can increase
- the menstrual cycle can become disturbed
- the digestive system can become upset; nausea can result
- the immune system becomes less effective
- fatigue and exhaustion can develop
- skin problems can develop such as dryness, rashes, blushing and acne
- speech can slow
- the face can flush or look pale.

In the mind:

- anxiety and nervousness can develop
- depression and moodiness can arise
- feelings of loneliness and isolation can develop
- emotional outbursts or uncharacteristic behaviour may occur
- concentration and decision-making can become difficult
- sensitivity to others can increase, particularly concerning perceived criticism
- situation avoidance can develop
- the desire for inactivity or excessive activity may arise
- over-dependence on stimulants or addictive behaviour may result.

Teacher Well-being: Looking after yourself and your career in the classroom suggests considering the following questions if you think that you might be suffering from negative stress. If you find yourself answering them positively, it is likely that you should talk to your chosen health care provider about how you are feeling and what you are experiencing:

- What do others say about you? How are you described?
- How do you interact with others? Are you patient and attentive or snappy and distracted?

- Are you less confident than you used to be? Shyer and more introspective?
- Is your mood stable and balanced or do you find yourself swinging from contentment to distress in one go?
- Is decision-making more difficult than it used to be and concentration a thing of the past?
- Are your thoughts generally positive or negative? Do you have any thoughts of impending doom? Are you tearful and depressed?
- Have your sleeping patterns changed? Do you find yourself waking at night, or else constantly tired and falling asleep at the first opportunity?
- Do you rely on stimulants more than usual? Has the occasional drink become a daily necessity? Are you smoking or smoking more than usual?
- Have there been changes to your eating habits? Is your appetite as it was?
- Has work taken over where leisure once reigned? Once you have completed your work do you have the energy for a full social life?
- What are your energy levels like? Do you experience the highs and lows of adrenaline 'dependence'?
- Are you constantly fighting low-level infections such as colds and sore throats? Are you suffering from headaches or aches in other parts of your body?
- Do you ever experience palpitations or waves of fear or panic?
- Are you able to distinguish between external and internal pressures?

The above lists are not exhaustive in any way but do serve to show that excessive stress can hit us in a variety of ways. We need to become self-aware so that we don't miss the warning signs that the body sends. Take action sooner rather than later. The quicker you deal with stress, the easier it is to get back to your usual self. If someone close to you has sensed a difference in you, it is probably time to take notice.

> The impact of stress is not to be taken lightly. We now know that it can contribute to a variety of serious illnesses and the sooner you take action to reduce stress and eliminate its negative symptoms, the better. Always consult your chosen health care provider if you think that you may be suffering from stress.

I had a panic attack at school the other day. I've never had one before and it was terrifying. I'm dreading another one happening. Is there anything I can do?

Panic attacks can be terrifying – there is no other way to describe them. Some people feel as though they really are going to die when in the throes of a panic attack.

One thing to take on board is that having a panic attack is evidence that excessive stress is taking its toll. It's important, therefore, to tackle the causes of this stress.

If you feel that another panic attack is about to happen, these ideas may help:

- Remember that this is a normal response to your body's heightened sense of fear.
- You can't die from a panic attack. The feelings that arise during them are just that – feelings.
- Repeat a calming affirmation to yourself when you sense that a panic attack may be on its way.
- Take time consciously to relax yourself. Go round the muscles in your body systematically and relax them.
- Don't think of the past or future – only the present matters.
- Go with what you are feeling and it will pass more quickly.
- Concentrate on keeping your breathing calm and measured.
- Recognise when the feelings of panic start to subside.

You're not alone if you suffer from panic attacks. Research suggests that as many as 10 per cent of adults experience at least one at some point in their lives. They don't need to become a feature of your life though, so do take steps to address what their cause may be for you.

Panic attacks are evidence of some pretty strong underlying disease and should be taken as a warning that all is not well. While they aren't life threatening in any way, you do need to find out their cause and take action to eliminate any obvious stressors. Your chosen health care provider should help you through this process. Don't think that you have to do this alone.

I am really struggling with the whole work–life balance thing. How do other teachers manage to have anything like a home life in their first year of teaching?

It's tough! But you're not alone. Many teachers in their first few years and beyond struggle with maintaining a decent work–life balance, and I'm willing to bet that there isn't a teacher in the land who hasn't taken work home with them at some point, if not on a regular basis.

The short answer to this is that you have to manage your time in order to *create* the space in which to rest and relax, catch up with friends and family and pursue your hobbies. Work out when you would ideally like to have guaranteed time for yourself. Are there certain evenings you'd like to be free to go out? What are your favourite parts of the weekend? Are there any times when you wouldn't mind working? Be sure to identify what you want the time for (and it's fine if you just want to relax!) and aim to block it off as sacred. Give yourself clear signals for the start and end of work and be firm about not letting work time bleed into your precious time off.

You can always ask someone to help you achieve this kind of work–life balance. Tell them your intentions and what they might be able to do to help you achieve it. Maybe they could send you a text at the time you say you'll stop working, or arrange to go out with you on certain nights of the week. It doesn't matter what your personal arrangements may be; what's important is that you focus on what it is that will encourage you to work efficiently when you're supposed to be working and to relax effectively when you're supposed to be relaxing! It may not be easy, but if you focus on *creating* a work–life balance, it will be far easier to achieve.

Other ideas to explore are whether you can reduce your workload by working collaboratively with a colleague or using resources that exist already in your school. Perhaps you can receive help with planning? Aim to create a wish list of exactly what it is that would make your life easier and don't be afraid to ask if there is anyone who you think could help you out.

There is more information on time management in Chapter 5 which you will find useful.

You can read much more about work–life balance in the book, *Teacher Well-being: Looking after yourself and your career in the classroom* (www.teacherwellbeing.info). The Teacher Support Network also carries extensive advice on looking after your work–life balance. See www.teachersupport.info for more details.

I'm starting to get symptoms of irritable bowel syndrome and my GP has told me that it's probably down to the stress of my job. I don't think I'm stressed though. Could I be stressed without realising it?

Yes, most certainly. Many people don't recognise the signs and symptoms of negative stress that our bodies give us. The trouble is that if we don't take steps to treat the stress signs sooner rather than later, they increase in intensity until we have no option but to take action (and then wonder what hit us!). It's not enough to treat our bodies symptomatically, we have to look at the whole picture of our lives and see what needs to be changed. Obliterating the pain of a headache with painkillers does nothing to sort out the cause of the headache and preventing it from occurring again in the future. With symptoms of IBS you could probably do with making sure you give your body the chance to eat and digest small quantities of good food regularly throughout the day. If you're one to eat 'on the hoof' or stop to take a bite only once the children have left at the end of the day, your digestive system (not to mention energy levels) are bound to suffer. Be sure to drink plenty of water throughout the day too because being properly hydrated can help your body to function smoothly.

It would be worth reading up on the signs of stress overload. Take a moment to visit the Teacher Support Network website: www.teachersupport.info. You may also find the following book useful, *Teacher Well-being: Looking after yourself and your career in the classroom* (www.teacherwellbeing.info).

I feel tired all the time. I wouldn't go as far as saying it's exhaustion, but I feel that I could sleep at any time! Is this usual?

Starting your first teaching job can be very draining both physically and emotionally, which can leave you feeling more tired than usual. This is a perfectly normal reaction to your change in circumstances and the feeling should diminish over time.

However, feelings of tiredness should be listened to, as they could be a symptom of an underlying condition that may require medical attention. Therefore, it is important to discuss how you feel with your health care provider. Do also make sure that you are doing all you can to ensure you get good quality sleep each night. These ideas may help:

- Camomile tea contains calming compounds and may help to induce sleep.
- Avoid caffeine (cut back slowly as it is addictive).
- Unwind before going to bed.
- Get into the habit of going to bed at a certain time.

- Make sure that your bedroom is as clutter-free and relaxing as possible.
- Speak to your health care provider if sleep still evades you.
- Try to get as many hours of sleep before midnight as possible.

I've been told that I'm a perfectionist! I don't want to lower my standards but I am aware that I do push myself hard. Any ideas on how to deal with this?

Perfectionism affects us all to some extent. Having a need for perfection in a job in which external factors can impact the way in which our plans go (for example, you may have the perfect lesson ready but the group is tired, it's the end of a busy week and they're just not as in to it as we'd hoped they would be) can be particularly difficult to handle.

There's nothing wrong with wanting to be the best you can be, but you do have to cut yourself a little slack. Being the best doesn't necessarily mean giving 200 per cent all the time. The demands you place on yourself have to be realistic if you're to maintain any sense of well-being.

Make sure that you give yourself a cut-off time when you are working. Know when to let a task go; you do not have to continue with it until you feel it is perfect if this level of commitment is having an adverse impact in other areas of your life. Also, think about how you interpret what is expected of you. Are you going the extra mile when it's not strictly necessary?

Keeping a check on perfectionism isn't about lowering standards. It's about being wise with your time and the degree of effort you expend, which has to be proportional to the task in hand. It's unlikely that you'll get to the point of feeling that all your tasks are complete; teaching just isn't that kind of job. Therefore it's going to be wise for you to find a way of being happy with doing things to the best of your ability in the time available. In the vast majority of cases, your best is going to be more than good enough, while perfection – whatever that may be – is likely to remain unattainable.

Above all else, perfectionism is not a particularly self-nurturing trait. If you can adjust your expectations of yourself when they drift out of hand, you'll enjoy a far more fulfilling working life.

CHAPTER 9

Personal issues

Confine yourself to the present.

(Marcus Aurelius)

Introduction

Beyond the day-to-day nitty-gritty of work in a school, issues can loom in a teacher's experience of life which need attention. At times, these issues can be overwhelming and lead to necessary intervention in order to ensure that well-being is maintained, while at other times it might simply be a temporary blip that is causing additional stress or anxiety. In addition, too, there are factors such as GTC registration, pay issues and union membership that may not contribute directly to your work as a teacher, but which necessarily take your time to set up.

Perhaps the most important thing to remember when facing personal issues as well as other aspects of the job beyond the classroom that require your attention is that you are *more* than a teacher. You may also be a parent, a partner, a son or daughter, a carer; you may need to maintain a social network of friends in order to hang on to some work–life balance or you may have commitments to voluntary projects outside school. Whatever you life entails, it's essential that you don't start to see yourself *solely* as a teacher. This is just one part, albeit a pretty major one, of who you are as a person and what you do with your time. It's your way of *making* a living, not your sole *reason* for living! Understanding this will help you to cope with the challenges that life can present and deal with them in your stride.

FAQs in this chapter cover:

- Feeling exhausted
- Wanting to leave the profession
- Leave of absence
- Work–life balance
- QTS issues
- The Register of Teachers
- The General Teaching Council
- Teacher Reference Numbers
- Choosing a teacher union
- Pension schemes
- Pay issues
- Continuing professional development
- Working overseas
- Notice periods for moving on

I feel exhausted. It's like I'm limping from day to day and just getting through each lesson feels like a major victory. I know I'm on auto-pilot and I'm not enjoying my teaching at all. Why can't I keep up?

Teaching can be exhausting. It's emotionally and physically demanding and if we're not careful, the results of that can creep up on us while we're unaware. Being able to handle consistently the demands of the job essentially means becoming self-observant. It's important to learn the signs and symptoms your body throws out before it reaches the point of exhaustion. Like the old adage, 'a stitch in time', taking a day off to rebuild your energy reserves sooner rather than later is a very wise thing to do.

Go and see your chosen health care provider and talk through your symptoms and how you are feeling emotionally. It may be that you really need some time off, or perhaps a course of appropriate treatment will be enough to boost you while you work. The important thing is to get professional advice on your state of health. Don't muddle on hoping to feel better in time. Get some support and aim to reduce your workload by doing the bare minimum for a week or so. Look for opportunities when you can nurture yourself, for example by having some early nights and eating some really good food, and put yourself first for a while. Small steps can bring about big changes, but you may need support through this. Above all else, know that you are not alone.

I really think I want to leave the profession. I haven't even completed a year and I just want to get out. I feel like a failure. What can I do?

Many teachers feel that they would like to leave the profession at some stage of their careers and it's fair to say that quite a hefty chunk consider leaving very early on in their careers. The retention of teachers is a big issue in developed countries across the world, not least because the job can be so physically and emotionally demanding.

You're right to acknowledge how you are feeling, but before thinking about the relatively extreme decision to leave the profession entirely, spend some time thinking about precisely what it is about your job that you find difficult to deal with. There are many sources of help out there for you and often, identifying key factors in an emotion helps us to see that exactly what is getting us down and what is supporting us.

Aim to identify exactly what is wrong and what you would like help with. For example, is behaviour an issue in your lessons? Are you struggling with your workload? Do you get on OK with your colleagues? Have your induction observations been going well or have development needs been identified? Create a list of perceived problems and think about who and what can help you with them. Don't try to tackle everything at once as that is a certain route to feeling overwhelmed. Once you have done this, take one issue at a time and resolve to do something right now towards improving things, even if that is as simple as having a conversation with your induction tutor to raise some concerns. Making that commitment to move things forward can relieve a huge amount of pressure as you are no longer 'victim'. Taking control and actively seeking help can often be enough to reinvigorate our enthusiasm.

However, if you don't feel that taking these steps will help you to work through what you're feeling now it may be that teaching isn't for you, in which case it would be a good idea to seek some careers advice as soon as possible. It's usually going to be a good idea to complete your induction period if at all possible so that if you do want to leave the profession, you can make a return more easily at a future date should you so decide.

Whatever happens, it's going to be more helpful for you to consider it as *change* rather than as *failure*. There is absolutely nothing wrong with realising that you would like to make a change in your life and taking steps to improve your sense of happiness and well-being.

Don't forget all the sources of help that are out there for you, which include:

- your induction tutor or other trusted colleagues
- your union
- the person within your LEA with responsibilities for NQTs (you should have been told who this is)
- the induction team at the DfES
- Teacher Support Line: 08000 562 561
- your GP or other health care provider
- NQT and Students Zone on www.eteach.com.

I have to move house and haven't been able to arrange for this to happen at a weekend. Am I entitled to having a day off for moving?

There are no *entitlements* for this kind of leave as such, but many schools will be supportive of events such as moving house on the understanding that it's usually a rare occurrence for a teacher.

It's up to your head teacher and governors to decide whether you can have a day off for moving. Write to them as soon as you know the details of the leave you require and explain the situation. In most cases, teachers are granted a day of *unpaid* leave at least. The more notice you can give the better.

I'm feeling really guilty over the way that my schoolwork takes over my entire life. It's really having an impact on my relationship with my partner and I've just started to realise the number of times I have to cancel arrangements just because I'm too tired or have too much to do. I can't see a way to change but we can't go on like this.

First of all, taking work home seems to be an inherent part of the job. That said, it shouldn't spill over into all corners of your home life and needs careful containment. It's not fair on either of you for it to dominate in this way so you do need to take action. Try keeping at least one full day free every weekend and have a very strict cut-off time on weekday evenings after which you do not work. It's also nice to arrange a 'date' once a week. This arrangement shouldn't be cancelled at the last minute – it's a priority! Make it into something that you can both look forward to. Even small steps like this show that you are willing to address the problem and will make you more aware of containing what you do outside school. It's all about limits and increasing your awareness of just what you can achieve when you know that your time is allocated. Start making changes now; it'll be worth it!

Someone told me that my QTS will run out. Is that the case?

No. Once you have QTS you have it permanently. It doesn't run out.

I'm not sure if I have QTS or not. How can I find out?

The GTC can give you this information. You can email the Teachers Qualifications Helpdesk: tqhelpdesk@gtce.org.uk or call: 0121 345 0140.

I can't find my QTS certificate anywhere. What can I do?

You can get an official letter from the GTC which confirms your QTS. If you need to do this, email: tqhelpdesk@gtce.org.uk or call: 0121 345 0140.

What is the 'Register of Teachers'?

The General Teaching Council for England has a statutory duty to maintain a Register of Teachers. All qualified teachers and supply teachers who want to teach in a maintained school or a non-maintained special school or pupil referral unit must register with the GTC by law. If you have a place on the Register it means that your qualification is guaranteed.

If you have any specific questions about registering with the GTC you can contact the Registration Helpdesk: registration@gtce.org.uk or call: 0870 001 0308.

Is the GTC the same as the GTCE?

When people refer to the GTC they usually mean the GTCE (General Teaching Council for England). Each of the countries in the UK has its own GTC, so there is also a GTCS (General Teaching Council for Scotland), a GTCW (General Teaching Council for Wales) and a GTCNI (General Teaching Council for Northern Ireland). So, technically, if you're referring to the GTC in England, it's the GTCE.

When do I have to join the General Teaching Council? I don't find out what my final grades are

until the end of July so do I join after I get confirmation of my qualified teacher status?

You just need to wait to be contacted. Your teacher training provider will inform the General Teaching Council that you have been awarded QTS. The GTC will then update its database and send you a certificate. In the mean time, you should have been given a form to complete by your college or university in order to allocate your DfES number. There's a box to tick on this form which will automatically register you for the GTC. This form then goes back to your college or university to be sent to the GTC. If you haven't seen this form yet, ask your tutor about it.

Should I have a GTCE registration number?

There isn't any such thing. If an employer or prospective employer wants to check whether you are registered they can do so with the GTC through their employer access.

What is a 'teacher reference number'?

The Teacher Reference Number is also sometimes known as the DfES number. These are allocated to trainee teachers when they start initial teacher training, but not all of these people will go on to secure qualified teacher status.

I'm not sure whether I'm registered with the GTC. How can I find out?

All you need to do is to ring the enquiry line and give your full name and date of birth. You may also be asked for your National Insurance number or your DfES number for more in-depth queries.

What teaching union should I join? I don't want to join anything that is political in any way so would I be better off not joining one at all?

It's really important to join a union, not only for the professional protection they offer members but also for the fact that they work to improve the conditions of employment for all teachers. All organisations are 'political' to a greater or lesser extent because politics pervades all our lives, but that does not detract from their effectiveness. Part of any union's remit is to act as a conduit between the workers and the government. In doing this they can influence policy in certain circumstances and encourage successive governments to make decisions that will serve their members best. When choosing a union make sure you consider all the options available to you and look not so much at the perks and benefits but at the actual levels of support that you can expect should you need professional help. At the very least you should expect:

- advice over work-related matters
- to be represented in discussions with employers
- to be offered welfare benefits, professional and personal legal assistance from an education law specialist, professional insurance and financial services
- confidential crisis support.

Ask plenty of questions of any union you are thinking of joining and choose wisely. Above all else, make sure you join one of them. Don't start your career without the support and insurance that a union can offer you.

I've heard that you should just join the union that is most popular in your school. Is that true?

I don't advocate that for several reasons, the most important being that you should join a union that best suits your ideas and philosophies. This means looking closely at what they *all* have to offer and making your decision based on that research rather than by following the crowd. And don't forget, too, that as you move on into your first job and then subsequently move schools through your career you're bound to belong to a union in the minority at some point and this does not matter. The most important thing is to choose wisely to suit *your* beliefs and *your* needs.

Once you've joined a union are you in it for life?

No. You can decide to leave and join another union if you want to (although it's probably not a good idea to leave one union and not join another). In reality, many people do stick with their original choice throughout their careers, but this isn't essential. You may like to look into what other unions have to offer you at various stages of your career, just to see if you'd be happier making a change.

How do I choose what union to join?

One way is to look at all the goodies and benefits they offer and see what you fancy, but that's unlikely to tell you much about how a union functions as an organisation, and the degree of support you can expect in a time of need. It's going to be far better to make sure that any union you are thinking of joining will promise to offer you *appropriate* help in good time as and when you need it.

The Newly Qualified Teacher's Handbook suggests asking questions on the following issues when deciding what union to join:

- At what stage will you be given *legally qualified* help from the union should you need it?
- Will any problems you may encounter be dealt with on a local, regional or national level?
- How responsible is the union for any advice that it gives you?
- Would you be entitled to seek a second opinion on your situation and any advice that you are given by the union if you feel it to be necessary? Would your case be dropped in this event?

The vast majority of teachers are satisfied with the level of support that they are given by their unions and in fact, many teachers go through their careers without encountering situations that require union intervention. That said, if you do need professional help and advice, your union could be invaluable so it is certainly worth taking some time to decide which one will be best for you.

You can find out much more about joining a union from *The Newly Qualified Teacher's Handbook*: www.nqthandbook.info. It is also worth looking at the websites of all the teacher unions:

- NUT: www.nut.org.uk
- NASUWT: www.teachersunion.org.uk
- ATL www.askatl.org.uk
- PAT: www.pat.org.uk

I'm in my early twenties so I don't need to think about joining the pension scheme yet do I? Are pensions all they're cracked up to be?

Pensions are still, despite all the uncertainty about them, thought to be the best way of saving for retirement and the earlier you can start saving the better. There have been news reports recently about using property to generate a retirement income but this is just as risky as the equity markets. If you want to explore other options, it really is best to do this in addition to paying into a pension fund such as the teachers' pension scheme (see below). However, it is important to get independent advice from a pensions specialist (who will almost certainly advise you to pay into the teachers' pension scheme). Check out your Yellow Pages for independent financial advisors in your area, or search on the internet for ideas. Be sure to choose one that is authorised and regulated by the Financial Services Authority. Find out more here: www.unbiased.co.uk

How can I find out more about the teachers' pension scheme (TPS)?

You should be told about the TPS by your school. All teachers are eligible to join (under certain conditions) and pay 6 per cent of their salary into the scheme. Employers currently contribute 13.5 per cent (making a total of 19.5 per cent). The TPS is what is described as a 'final salary scheme' meaning that your pension would be based on your final salary before retirement.

> You can find out more about the TPS from the following website: www.teacherspensions.co.uk or by ringing 0845 6066166.

I don't understand my pay slip. It looks to me like I'm paying too much tax. Is there anything I can do?

If you get in touch with your LEA's payroll department they will be able to go through your payslip and explain what it all means. They can differ from LEA to LEA so it is well worth asking direct if there is anything that you don't understand.

Any questions about your tax code can be answered by HM Revenue and Customs, which is the government department responsible for the business of the former Inland Revenue and HM Customs and Excise. It's worth having a good look through the contacts page on its website (listed below) and there is a leaflet available online and in your local tax office called *Understanding Your Tax Code*, which will tell you all you need to know.

> You can find out more about taxation from the HM Revenue and Customs website: www.hmrc.gov.uk.

Although I'm an NQT I have got five years' experience of working in private industry. I thought I'd be paid more than the basic starting salary for new teachers but I'm not. Is there anything I can do about it?

It is entirely up to your school's governing body to decide what point you should be placed on when you start your job. Some will want to reward previous experience by placing you higher than M1 on the main pay scale while others may not have the flexibility in their budget to do that.

It is worth contacting your union to see what point you might be placed on in an ideal world. You could then talk to your head teacher (or ask your union to do this on your behalf) to ask if he or she would consider putting your case to the governing body.

I don't understand the teaching pay scales. How are they structured?

Teachers are paid on a main pay scale which has six points, M1–M6. NQTs usually start at the bottom of the scale on M1 but, with relevant experience, they may start higher up the scale. It is up to individual schools to decide on the award of additional points for experience and this will be explained in your school's pay policy. Typically teachers move through the main scale at the rate of one point per year.

There is also an upper pay scale which runs from U1 to U3. Your progression to the upper pay scale is performance based and movement through the scale is usually at the rate of one point every two years.

Head teachers and other senior staff are paid on a forty-three point leadership spine.

If you are liable to pay the General Teaching Council fee you will receive a one-off payment, currently £33, each year.

The School Teachers' Pay and Conditions Document is published once a year and it sets out teachers' terms and conditions of service. It contains everything you need to know about your working time arrangements and professional duties and can be viewed on Teachernet (see below).

Other issues such as maternity leave, notice periods and sick pay have been negotiated and agreed between trade unions and employers. You can get further information on these from your school and from your LEA.

You can find out more about teachers' pay from Teachernet: www.teachernet.gov.uk/pay.

I'm coming to the end of my induction period so is that it for my professional development? Do I just get on with teaching now?

Not at all! You're only just beginning! It doesn't matter how much or how little experience you have as a teacher, continuing professional development is *always* going to be relevant.

There is a great section of Teachernet which can help you to plan for your own CPD needs at every stage of your career. It will be well worth taking the time to study the information found at the link given below where you will also find a professional and career development support tool designed to show you how you might progress along your chosen career pathway. The more you can absorb the notion of lifelong learning, the more you will be able to get out of your time spent in the teaching profession!

Find out more about continuing professional development here: www.teachernet.gov.uk/professionaldevelopment/. There is also extensive information about CPD on the Training and Development Agency for Schools website: www.tda.gov.uk.

I'm considering taking some time out to do some voluntary work overseas. Would I be able to keep my job so I have something to come back to?

This depends entirely on your school's governing body. Some are very keen to support staff who want to take part in such ventures because they can lead to such a broadening of experience for teachers, which can then be brought back into the classroom. They also appreciate that if teachers have their heart set on working abroad for a period, it's probably not a good idea to try to persuade them otherwise!

Find out how receptive your school is to your taking time out by talking to your head teacher about the possibility of a period of unpaid leave. Ultimately the governing body would have the final say on this but it's definitely worth asking. If you are granted unpaid leave, your post would probably be filled temporarily and you would be able to take it up again on your return. If you can find some positive benefits that you propose to bring back into the school (for example specific skills that you aim to learn) your request is more likely to be favourably received.

If you are not granted unpaid leave, don't let this put you off pursuing your dreams. Your skills may well be in high demand on your return, although there is no guarantee of being able to walk into work unless your job has been kept open for you.

> A good starting point for finding out more about teaching overseas as a volunteer is the Voluntary Service Overseas website: www.vso.org.uk. For information on teacher exchanges, the British Council website is a good source of information: www.britishcouncil.org/learning-fulbright.htm.

I'd like to move schools after I've completed my induction period. How much notice do I have to give?

Notice periods are agreed between employers and teacher unions and are explained in the Conditions of Service for School Teachers in England. Typically teachers resign at three dates through the school year, giving half a term's notice. These are around the end of October, the end of February and the end of May. That said, it is important to check your contract for exact details of how much notice you have to give when you want to leave your job.

> For more information about the Conditions of Service for School Teachers in England visit the Employers' Organisation for Local Government website: www.lg-employers.gov.uk.

CHAPTER 10

Hot education topics

To teach is to learn twice.

(Joseph Joubert)

Introduction

One thing that you'll quickly come to realise while you work as a teacher is that things change! The profession is in a constant state of development, and necessarily so. It would be highly undesirable for things to become static, nothing shifting, no new ideas and initiatives flowing into the ring. We need new ideas, developments and initiatives to ensure that education responds to the changing needs of society and, perhaps most importantly, of the children in our classes. But if we feel swamped, or that we can't keep up with new initiatives, we won't be able to utilise new learning in our lessons.

The key here is to keep an eye on the education news but not feel that it is vitally necessary for every new idea to be incorporated into your work. Be aware of what is going on in your field, and open to developments that could help you or the children you teach, but don't become obsessed with being bang up to date at all times if that means becoming so stressed out you cease to function effectively as a teacher! Rest assured, you will be told of all the initiatives that it is essential for you to be aware of. Take a relaxed attitude to keeping abreast of the world of education and you're more likely to be able to utilise what you discover and hear about.

This chapter looks at some of the main hot topics that you're likely to encounter in your first few years in the profession. One key thing to keep in mind is that just about every initiative or new idea that you may have to get to grips with will be geared towards raising standards of achievement. Some will be top-down initiatives and some will be grassroots movements, but the overall goals are usually to improve the standards of attainment of the children in our schools.

FAQs in this chapter cover:

- Keeping up with new ideas and initiatives
- Workforce remodelling
- Extended schools
- Higher level teaching assistants (HLTAs)
- Brain Gym®
- Emotional literacy
- e-consultations
- Common Transfer File
- Creativity
- Personalised learning
- Learning mentors
- Thinking skills
- Leading Edge Partnership Programme

How can I make sure that I keep up with new ideas and initiatives?

There are a number of sources of information beyond what you may be given in your school. These ideas will help, but don't feel that you need to rush off and bookmark every site! Just pay them a visit every now and then to see what's there for you or what you can make use of.

www.bbc.co.uk

Click on 'news' and then 'education' for all the latest news stories cross-referenced with relevant stories from the past too. These pages are updated all day every day so they really do carry the very latest education news.

www.teachernet.gov.uk

This is the government's website for teachers and it's packed with news, articles, information on, for example, professional development, research, whole school issues such as behaviour, and much more. It also has an online community and access to online publications relevant to your work. Teachernet is well worth getting to know and visiting regularly when you have a minute or two. It has an immense amount on it – too much to do justice to in this short paragraph!

www.schoolsweb.gov.uk/locate

SchoolsWeb Locate is an online directory which carries a huge amount of information on schools-related topics found on DfES websites. It's a way in to the array of information out there that may be useful to you.

www.standards.dfes.gov.uk

The DfES Standards website is all about raising standards, as you may guess. Here you'll find information about the latest government initiatives as well as advice, case studies and much more.

www.eteach.com

Although you'll probably be familiar with Eteach if you have been looking for a job, there's plenty more than just vacancies listed on the site. Eteach also carries extensive information on getting jobs and moving jobs, as well as its very busy, fully moderated online staff-room where you can pose questions and receive almost instant answers as well as take part in lively debates about hot education topics. The weekly newsletter offers a round-up of education news and much more.

www.teachers.tv

This is the television channel (available at the time of writing on Sky Guide, Telewest, ntl, KIT, HomeChoice and Freeview) for teachers. Programmes are either general to all teachers or specifically for primary or secondary teachers. If you don't have a chance to watch any of the programmes, the website is well worth browsing to see what's there for you.

Newspapers

The print media carry education news stories and some carry education supplements on certain days of the week.

What exactly is workforce remodelling?

As a teacher who is new to the profession, the concept of workforce remodelling won't mean much because you will already be joining a remodelled workforce. Most of the major changes have already been implemented. That said, more could follow and it's important to be aware of the ways in which your profession is developing.

In January 2003 a national agreement on tackling workload was signed; this introduced significant changes to teachers' conditions of service. The national agreement was in acknowledgement of the fact that workload was repeatedly cited as a major reason for leaving the profession, and that prior to the agreement, over 30 per cent of a teacher's working week was spent on non-teaching activities. The changes were implemented in three annual phases starting in September 2003.

You can find out more about workforce remodelling from www.remodelling.org.

What are 'extended schools'?

Extended schools are described on the remodelling website (www.remodelling.org) as schools which provide 'a range of services and activities often beyond the school day to help meet the needs of its pupils, their families and the wider community'. Many schools offer activities either on or around school grounds above and beyond the compulsory school day. This may be in partnership with other organisations such as private companies offering specific activities or voluntary organisations. The government's vision, as detailed on the remodelling website, is that for the primary phase, the notion of the extended school means:

• a range of study support activities: sports, arts, music, homework clubs, etc.
• parenting support opportunities, including family learning
• swift and easy referral from every school to a range of specialised support services for pupils
• childcare available at least 8am to 6pm, term time and school holidays.

And for the secondary phase, extended school means:

• study support activities: arts, music, opportunities to complete homework or coursework
• parenting support opportunities, including family learning
• swift and easy referral to a range of specialised pupil support services
• there may be scope for multi-agency teams on site
• a 'youth offer': a range of before and after school and holiday activities to engage young people

- opening up ICT, sports and arts facilities for use by the wider community.

It is highly likely that the school in which you teach will offer its pupils extended activities so it's useful to know exactly what's on offer and how your pupils benefit. You may even want to become involved yourself!

> You can find out more about extended schools from www.remodelling.org.

I've been told I'm going to have a higher level teaching assistant working with me in my class. How do they differ from other teaching assistants?

Higher level teaching assistants are teaching assistants who have been specifically trained to meet HLTA standards. They can be considered as 'senior support staff' and some who have achieved HLTA status may decide to go on to achieve qualified teacher status. There are thirty-one HLTA standards and these are divided under the headings of Professional Values and Practice, Knowledge and Understanding, and Teaching and Learning Activities.

One important point to keep in mind is that when you work with any support staff in your classroom, including HLTAs, you, as the teacher, are always the one to direct and supervise. However, the Training and Development Agency for Schools states that it is up to head teachers and/or teachers to decide whether the class teacher needs to be present in the classroom when HLTAs are working with children. It is therefore important that you discuss with all concerned exactly how you and your HLTA can maximise the benefit of your working relationship. Don't take anything for granted — if in doubt, talk to your head teacher and HLTA.

> You can find out more about higher level teaching assistants on the Training and Development Agency for Schools website: www.tda.gov.uk

What is Brain Gym®?

Brain Gym® is described as a movement-based educational programme. It aims to bring together the brain, senses and body so that the person doing Brain Gym® is ready to learn as effectively as possible. It is sometimes referred to as educational kinesiology and is certainly gaining in popularity in the UK. Brain Gym® is said to help children to improve their academic skills, memory and concentration, physical coordination and balance and self-development among other things.

There are several useful books written on Brain Gym® and its associated theories and a search on an internet search engine will throw up all sorts of sites devoted to the subject. Before disappearing off to the nearest computer, do ask in your school if any teachers are using Brain Gym® and whether they can share resources and ideas with you.

> You can find out more about Brain Gym® in the UK from the following website: www.braingym.org.uk.

I went for an interview and was asked about how I might develop my pupils' emotional literacy. I'm not exactly sure what that is! Any ideas?

Emotional literacy has been defined by Antidote (see below) as:

> the practice of interacting with others in ways that build understanding of our own and others' emotions, then using this understanding to inform our actions.

Schools can be particularly effective in developing young people's emotional literacy through close attention to relationships between pupils, between teachers and pupils as well as between teachers themselves. An emotionally literate school is not one in which cross words are never uttered, or emotions don't run high. Rather, it is one where the feelings of its community members are fully appreciated and taken into consideration as far as possible. When disagreements do arise, they are dealt with effectively and learned from for the future.

> You can find out much more about emotional literacy and what it means in schools from the Antidote website: www.antidote.org.uk. Antidote was set up by a diverse group who seek to 'apply the latest understandings of human nature to the challenge of creating a healthier and more sustainably prosperous society.' In addition, Optimus Professional Learning runs fully interactive professional development courses for teachers on emotional literacy and the emotionally literate school. See www.optimusprolearning.co.uk for further details.

Someone mentioned that it's possible for teachers to respond to government consultations. How can you find out more about them?

At any one time there are numerous government consultations on various topics and issues and teachers are welcome to submit their responses. You can find a full list of live e-consultations on the website listed below, as well as archived consultations and the results of consultations now closed. If you really get into the idea of responding to e-consultations to help shape the future of the profession, you can register to receive email updates when new consultations are published.

While you may not have a huge amount of time to devote to responding to e-consultations, this is an effective way of making your voice heard on matters that are important to your profession. They're certainly worth taking an interest in, if not taking part in.

> You can find out more about the process of e-consultation from the
> following website: www.dfes.gov.uk/consultations/.

I've heard the term 'Common Transfer File' mentioned. What does it mean? Is it something I should know about?

The Common Transfer File (or CTF as it is sometimes known) contains information about a child's previous performance. Wherever
the child goes, the CTF goes too, so that the new school has all the
relevant information about the child. The CTF must be transferred
to the new school within fifteen days of the child leaving (or ceasing
to be registered there). Since 2005, it has been a requirement that
this be done electronically.

As a new teacher, you may not come across CTFs unless you teach a
group that has just transferred from another school or when a new
pupil arrives in one of your classes.

> You can find out more about the CTF on www.teachernet.gov.uk.

Why do I keep hearing about creativity and the creative classroom? How can I find out more?

This has become a buzz issue over recent years and seems to have
become synonymous with livening up what happens in your classroom and encouraging excellence through a wide range of activities
linked to your curriculum area or age range. In this way, just about
anything can be taught through skills such as storytelling, drama
techniques, artwork, music as well as alternative methodologies in
addition to more traditional ways of imparting knowledge and
encouraging learning. The key is to consider what might encourage
risk-taking, innovation, imagination, invention, originality and so
on. The National Curriculum in Action website states that creativity

in the classroom is important because it helps pupils to think creatively and independently and to become

- more interested in discovering things for themselves
- more open to new ideas
- keen to work with others to explore ideas
- willing to work beyond lesson time when pursuing an idea or vision.

Creativity is thought to improve pupils' self-esteem as well as their levels of achievement and attainment. For this reason, a focus on creativity in the classroom is thought to be an incredibly enriching thing for both teachers and their students.

There is much more on creativity in the classroom at the National Curriculum in Action website: www.ncaction.org.uk/creativity/.

What is personalised learning? I've heard it mentioned in staff meetings but I'm not entirely sure what it is.

Personalised learning is part of a wider government strategy of personalisation across all of the public services. In short, as far as education is concerned, it's about helping children to reach their full potential within the learning context that they find themselves in. It isn't to be confused with individualised learning and one-to-one tuition. Personalised learning is about the way in which children learn as individuals who are part of a class with a class teacher. It is learning which meets the needs of pupils.

It may sound like there is jargon to become familiar with and initiatives to get on top of, but really, personalisation is a fairly simple concept that is being delivered already as part of a range of National Strategies such as Gifted and Talented, Every Child Matters, School Workforce Remodelling, ICT and the E-Learning Strategy and Schools for the Future.

> You can find out more about personalised learning and all of the strategies mentioned above from the government's Standards website: www.standards.dfes.gov.uk.

How can I find out more about learning mentors?

Learning mentors originated as one of the three main *Excellence in Cities* strands. They work in both the primary and secondary and the government's Standards website describes them as

- salaried staff who work with school and college students and pupils to help them address barriers to learning
- a bridge across academic and pastoral support roles with the aim of ensuring that individual pupils and students engage more effectively in learning and achieve appropriately
- a key ingredient in many school and college approaches to improve the achievement levels of pupils and students.

Learning mentors form a distinct occupational group quite separate from, although obviously linked to, teachers.

> You can find out more about learning mentors from the government's Standards website: www.standards.dfes.gov.uk.

I've been told to focus on thinking skills when I'm teaching. I thought I already was! What does it mean?

The notion of thinking skills is explicitly included in the National Curriculum and many schools will enhance this by asking staff to pay special attention to the development of thinking skills in the classroom. For some teachers this simply means a heightened awareness of the opportunities that exist to stretch thinking skills as a natural extension to the activities their children take part in. For others, however, they may be following a specific programme or approach that the whole school has signed up to. If this is the case in your school you should be told exactly what it entails, what your role is and precisely how it enables thinking skills to be developed through your work.

There are many books available for teachers on developing thinking skills in students. The internet is also a great source of information. It is thought that there are three main categories of approach to developing thinking skills. The DfES Standards website identifies these as being:

- cognitive intervention approaches
- brain based learning approaches
- philosophical approaches.

These approaches naturally overlap and occupy some common ground. If it's a topic that interests you, and let's face it, the development of thinking skills probably does interest most teachers, it's well worth taking a little time to see what's out there and how it may enhance your work in the classroom.

A great place to start your research on thinking skills is the government's Standards website. It has case studies, a glossary of terms, guidance and overviews of different approaches and much more. Although its main focus is thinking skills in the primary classroom, there's plenty of food for thought for secondary teachers too. Visit www.standards.dfes.gov.uk for further information.

The school I'm going to be teaching in is in a Leading Edge Partnership Programme. What is that?

Leading Edge Partnerships are groups of secondary schools (including special schools), headed by a lead school, which work together to tackle some of the tougher problems faced in the area. The aim behind the partnerships is to drive up standards. Funding is available for this collaborative work. Partnering often helps schools that may be struggling with the issues they face. Although this is primarily for secondary schools, it is possible for primary schools to partner secondary schools in the programme.

As far as you and your work in the school is concerned, you should be told exactly what the partnership means for you and precisely how you and your students may benefit. Your induction tutor or head teacher will be able to tell you more.

You can find out more about the Leading Edge Partnership Programme from the Standards website: www.standards.dfes.gov.uk.

Jargon buster

ACE	Advisory Centre for Education www.ace-ed.org.uk
ACE	Arts Council for England www.artscouncil.org.uk
ACPC	Area Child Protection Committee
ACW	Arts Council for Wales www.acw-ccc.org.uk
AD(H)D	attention deficit (hyperactivity) disorder
AEB	Associated Examining Board www.aeb.org.uk
AGCAS	Association of Graduate Careers Advisory Services www.agcas.org.uk/
AHRB	Arts and Humanities Research Board www.ahrb.ac.uk/
AHT	assistant head teacher
ALS	additional literacy support
AP	action plan
APL	accreditation of prior learning
APS	Alliance of Parents and Schools
AQA	Assessment and Qualifications Alliance www.aqa.org.uk
ASD	autistic spectrum disorder www.nas.org.uk
AST	advanced skills teacher www.standards.dfes.gov.uk/ast/
AT	attainment target
ATL	Association of Teachers and Lecturers www.askatl.org.uk
BEACO	behaviour and attendance coordinator (in secondary schools)

BECTA	British Educational Communication and Technology Agency www.becta.org.uk
BESTS	behaviour education support teams www.dfes.gov.uk/behaviourandattendance
BETT	British education and teaching technology www.becta.org.uk/
BIP	behaviour improvement programme
BSA	Basic Skills Agency www.basic-skills.co.uk
BSP	behaviour support plan
CAA	computer assisted assessment
CAL	computer assisted learning
CAMHS	Child and Adolescent Mental Health Services www.youngminds.org.uk/camhs/
CATs	cognitive ability tests
CBEVE	Central Bureau for Educational Visits and Exchanges
CDC	Council for Disabled Children www.ncb.org.uk/cdc/
CEDC	Community Education Development Centre www.continyou.org.uk/
CEDP	Career Entry and Development Profile
CEG	careers education and guidance
CEO	chief education officer
CILT	Centre for Information on Language Teaching and Research www.cilt.org.uk/
CLPE	Centre for Language in Primary Education www.clpe.co.uk/
CPD	continuing professional development
CPI	child protection issue
CPS	common pay scale
CRAC	Careers Research and Advisory Centre www.crac.org.uk/
CRB	Criminal Records Bureau www.crb.gov.uk/
CRE	Commission for Racial Equality www.cre.gov.uk/
C School	county school
CTC	city technology college
CTF	Common Transfer File
D&T	design and technology

DENI	Department of Education for Northern Ireland www.deni.gov.uk/
DfES	Department for Education and Skills www.dfes.gov.uk/
DHT	deputy head teacher
DLOs	desirable learning outcomes
DPC	Data Protection Commission www.informationcommissioner.gov.uk/
DRC	Disability Rights Commission www.drc-gb.org/
EA	external assessor
EAL	English as an additional language
EAZ	education action zone
EBD	emotional and behavioural difficulties
EBP	education business partnership
EDP	education development plan
Edubase	database of educational establishments in England and Wales www.edubase.gov.uk/Index.aspx
EECs	early excellence centres www.literacytrust.org.uk/ database/earlyex.html
EFL	English as a foreign language
EFS	educational formula spending
EHWB	emotional health and well-being
EiC	Excellence in Cities www.standards.dfes.gov.uk/sie/eic/
ELCs	eLearning Credits
ELGs	early learning goals
ELWa	Education and Learning Wales www.elwa.org.uk/
EMA	education maintenance allowance
ERIC	everyone reading in class
ESL	English as a second language
ESO	education supervision order
ESOL	English as a second or other language
ESW	education social worker
EWO	education welfare officer
EY	early years
EYDCP	Early Years Development Childcare Partnerships www.surestart.gov.uk/
FAS	Funding Agency for Schools

FASNA	Foundation and Aided Schools National Association www.fasna.org.uk
FE	further education
FEFC	further education funding council
FEI	further education institution
FHE	Further and Higher Education
FOI	freedom of information
FS	feeder schools
FSA	Food Standards Agency www.food.gov.uk/
FSM	free school meals
FTE	full-time equivalent
FTET	full-time education and training
GB	governing body
GPT	guaranteed planning time
GRTP	graduate and registered teacher programmes
GT	gifted and talented
GTCE	General Teaching Council for England www.gtce.org.uk/
GTCNI	General Teaching Council for Northern Ireland www.gtcni.org.uk
GTCS	General Teaching Council for Scotland www.gtcs.org.uk
GTCW	General Teaching Council for Wales www.gtcw.org.uk
GTP	graduate teacher programme
GTTR	Graduate Teacher Training Registry www.gttr.ac.uk/
HE	higher education
HEA	health education authority
HEI	higher education institution
HI	hearing impaired
HLTA	higher level teaching assistant
HMCI	Her Majesty's Chief Inspector of Schools
HMI	Her Majesty's inspectors
HoD	head of department
HoS	head of school
HoY	head of year
HSE	Health and Safety Executive www.hse.gov.uk/

HSI	Healthy Schools Initiative
HT	head teacher
IAP	individual action plan
IC	information commissioner
	www.informationcommissioner.gov.uk
ICG	Institute of Careers Guidance www.icg-uk.org/
ICT	information and communications technology
IEP	individual education plan
IiP	Investors in People www.investorsinpeople.co.uk
IiYP	Investors in Young People
ILP	information and learning technology
INSET	in-service education and training
IRT	identification referral and tracking
ISC	Independent Schools Council www.isc.co.uk/
ITE	initial teacher education
ITT	initial teacher training
IWB	interactive white board
JMI	junior, middle and infant
KS	key stage
LD	level description
LEA	local education authority
LSA	learning support assistant
LSAC	Language, Sports and Arts Colleges
LSC	Learning and Skills Council www.lsc.gov.uk
LSP	learning strategy partnership
LSU	learning support unit
MA	modern apprenticeships www.apprenticeships.org.uk/
MFL	modern foreign languages
MLD	moderate/mild learning difficulties
MNS	maintained nursery school
NAACE	National Association of Advisors for Computers in Education www.naace.org/
NACCCE	National Advisory Committee on Creative and Cultural Education
NACCEG	National Advisory Council for Careers and Educational Guidance

NACE	National Association for Able Children in Education www.nace.co.uk/
NACETT	National Advisory Council on Education and Training Targets
NAGC	National Association for Gifted Children www.nagc.org
NAPCE	National Association for Pastoral Care in Education www.napce.org.uk
NAS	National Autistic Society www.nas.org.uk
NASEN	National Association for Special Educational Needs www.nasen.org.uk/
NASUWT	National Association of Schoolmasters/Union of Women Teachers www.teachersunion.org.uk/
NATSOC	National Society for Promoting Religious Education www.natsoc.org.uk/
NC	National Curriculum www.ncaction.org.uk/
NCET	National Council for Educational Technology
NCPTA	National Confederation of Parent Teacher Associations www.ncpta.org.uk/
NCS	National Childcare Strategy
NCT	National Curriculum Test (see NTs)
NEOST	National Employers' Organisation for School Teachers www.lg-employers.gov.uk
NFER	National Foundation for Educational Research www.nfer.ac.uk/index.cfm
NGfL	National Grid for Learning www.ngfl.gov.uk/
NHSS	National Healthy Schools Standard www.wiredforhealth.gov.uk/
NLS	National Literacy Strategy www.standards.dfes.gov.uk/ literacy
NLT	National Literacy Trust www.literacytrust.org.uk
NNS	National Numeracy Strategy www.standards.dfes. gov.uk/numeracy
NOF	New Opportunities Fund www.nof.org.uk/
NoR	number on roll
NQT	newly qualified teacher
NTs	National Tests (often called SATs)

NUT	National Union of Teachers www.teachers.org.uk/
ODPM	Office of the Deputy Prime Minister
OECD	Organisation for Economic Cooperation and Development www.oecd.org/
Ofsted	Office for Standards in Education www.ofsted.gov.uk/
OSHL	out of school hours learning
OTT	overseas trained teacher
PAFT	parents as first teachers
PANDA	performance and assessment data
PAT	Professional Association of Teachers www.pat.org.uk/
PAT	pupil achievement tracker
PE	physical education
PEP	personal education plan
PFI	private finance initiative
PI	performance indicators
PM	performance management
PMLD	profound and multiple learning difficulties
PNS	Primary National Strategy
PNW	Pupil Needs Weighting
PoS	programme of study
PPA	planning, preparation and assessment
PPP	public private partnership
PROLOG	DfES publishing department 0845 6022260, dfes@prolog.uk.com
PRP	performance related pay
PRU	pupil referral unit
PSA	parent staff association
PSE	personal and social education
PSHE	personal, social and health education
PSLD	physical and severe learning difficulties
PSP	pastoral support programme
PT	part time
PTA	parent teacher association
PTR	pupil teacher ratio
QCA	Qualifications and Curriculum Authority www.qca.org.uk

QTS	qualified teacher status
RE	religious education
REEF	Race Employment and Education Forum
RgI/RI	registered inspector
SAC	Scottish Arts Council www.scottisharts.org.uk
SACRE	Standing Advisory Council on Religious Education
SAI	School Access Initiative
SATs	see NTs
SCD	severe communication difficulties
SCE	Service Children's Education
SCITT	school centred initial teacher training
SDP	school development plan
SEN	special educational needs
SENCO	special educational needs coordinator
SLC	Student Loans Company www.slc.co.uk/
SLD	severe learning difficulties
SLDD	students with learning difficulty and/or disability
SLT	senior leadership team
SMSC	spiritual, moral, social and cultural development
SMT	senior management team
SRE	sex and relationship education
SRS	safer routes to school
SSD	social services department
SSE	school self-evaluation
STRB	school teachers' review body
TA	teaching assistant
TC	technology college
TDA	Training and Development Agency for Schools www.tda.gov.uk/
TEC	Training and Enterprise Council
TESSS	The Extended Schools Support Service www.continyou.org.uk/
TPS	teachers' pension scheme www.teacherspensions.co.uk/
UNESCO	United Nations Educational, Scientific and Cultural Organisation www.unesco.org

VA school	voluntary aided school
VC school	voluntary controlled school
VI	visually impaired
VLE	virtual learning environment
VTC	virtual teacher centre
WAMG	Workforce Agreement Monitoring Group

Index